Vessels of Evil

VESSELS OF EVIL

American Slavery and the Holocaust

LAURENCE MORDEKHAI THOMAS

TEMPLE UNIVERSITY PRESS

Philadelphia

Temple University Press, Philadelphia 19122
Copyright © 1993 by Temple University. All rights reserved
Published 1993
Printed in the United States of America

⊗ The paper used in this publication meets the minimum requirements
of American National Standard for Information Sciences—Permanence
of Paper for Printed Library Materials, ANSI Z39.48-1984

Library of Congress Cataloging-in-Publication Data

Thomas, Laurence, 1949–
    Vessels of evil : American slavery and the Holocaust / Laurence
Mordekhai Thomas.
        p.   cm.
    Includes index.
    ISBN 1-56639-093-1
    1. Slavery—United States.   2. Holocaust, Jewish (1939–1945)
I. Title.
F441.T47   1993
940.53′18′0973—dc20   93-12386

To Shimon Brand—a mensch

Contents

Preface

Since my early teenage years, I have thought about the experiences of blacks and Jews. My thoughts developed over the years, but I generally kept my opinions to myself. I probably never would have written this book but for an invitation I received from Alan Rosenberg and Gerald E. Meyers to contribute to their collection, *Echoes from the Holocaust* (Philadelphia: Temple University Press, 1989).

My aim in this book has been to paint with a broad brush a picture of the hostile experiences of blacks and Jews—taking the Holocaust for Jews and American Slavery for blacks as watershed historical experiences. My aim has not been to say anything new about the history and experiences of either Jews or blacks, but simply to make sense of what is unshakably there. More precisely, my concern in this work has been to articulate with both sensitivity and rigor the differences between the hostile experiences of Jews and blacks. This book, then, is not a historical work; for, as I have said, it assumes what is unshakably there. To revisionists, I have nothing to say, anyway. What could be said?

On the other hand, this book is very much a philosophical work, though traditional philosophical issues are not explicitly taken up here. But nothing has more animated my thinking about traditional philosophical issues than the concerns of this book. For example, most discussions of the difference between acts and omissions have revolved around highly artificial examples. Needless to say, the discussion becomes very real indeed when applied to American Slavery and the Holocaust. This is a philosophical work because I seek to offer a rigorous analysis of the differences between the hostile experiences of blacks and Jews. Doing so has sometimes meant making sense of concepts, attitudes, and labels that are unshakably there.

My hope is that this work will offer some insight into the differences between the watershed historical experiences of Jews and blacks—the Holocaust and American Slavery. From there, I hope that some insight can be gained into the differences between the ways in which Jews and blacks have gone on to survive. I mean to say considerably more than what many might think obvious, namely that Jews as a people have flourished more than blacks as a people—at least in North America.

Difference is not a virtue in and of itself. But there can be no true understanding of a people without a proper grasp of its moral pain. I aim for a proper grasp of the moral pain of both Jews and blacks. I write with the conviction that the moral pain of neither can be subsumed under nor assimilated into the moral pain of the other.

It must be emphasized, however, that my aim is to articulate the conceptual differences between the Holocaust and American Slavery rather than to compare the atrocities of one with the other. These have been well documented by numerous others, and I have nothing to add. I have tried to capture the overarching structure—the general social pattern, if you will—of these institutions; and I am fully aware that one can always find an incident that would be at odds with my account. However, that would be true of any account. But the plausible case for a pattern is not defeated by special incidents. At any rate, for a concise statement of the differences between the two institutions under discussion, see the penultimate paragraph of Section 16.

In keeping with a long-standing tradition of philosophical thought, a most relevant consideration to the tone of this work is the following: Though, to be sure, I have tried to be true to the judgment that the Holocaust and American Slavery were both notoriously evil institutions, I have done so, however, by focusing only upon the bare essentials of culpability needed to be compatible with that judgment. This hardly downplays the wrong of these institutions; for if the judgment holds when only the bare essentials are considered, then a fortiori it will hold when these institutions are considered in the full measure of their culpability. The issue is not whether I have left out details of horror that one would have liked included but whether, in the end, I have been true to the judgment that American Slavery and the Holocaust were the morally horrendous institutions that we, as decent people, rightly take them to be.

As I presented various parts of this book around the country, nothing intrigued me more than the extent to which individual blacks and individual Jews would take just about any remark by me that one group did not suffer in the way that the other group suffered as evidence that I was arguing that one group had suffered less than the other in terms of American Slavery and the Holocaust. In fact, in the expectation that I might be warming up to an invidious comparison, there were times when people heard what I simply did not say, and would never have thought to say. But this observation is not quite right: More often than not, an outspoken person did not mind an invidious comparison at all, so long as it turned out that the group to which she or he belonged had suffered the most! I was a disappointment to such individuals in the audience. So, too, will I be a disappointment to anyone seeking a like conclusion in this book regarding American Slavery and the Holocaust.

When, at the invitation of Alan Rosenberg and Gerald E. Meyers, I wrote "Liberalism and the Holocaust" for their collection,[1] I never imagined that I would one day write this book. Indeed, I would have balked at the very suggestion. I would not even have accepted their invitation had it not been for the promptings of Norman Care of Oberlin College. In any case, my fulfilling that obligation broke a dam, as it were, and things were never the same afterward. Next came "Jews, Blacks, and Group Autonomy," followed by "American Slavery and the Holocaust." The latter article grew out of a course of the same title that I decided to teach in the fall of 1988 at Oberlin College. The course was a most profound experience. I could not have asked for a better group of students. By semester's end, I was somehow morally committed to writing this book. In the meantime, a draft of the paper "American Slavery and the Holocaust" was circulating, and requests to present it here and there were pouring in. While all the presentations bore that title, or something close to it, the truth of the matter is that I never presented quite the same paper twice. I was writing this book in spite of myself!

By the fall of 1989, I found myself holding a professorship at Syracuse University and attending Young Israel Sharei Torah. At those two places I met the scholars Alan Berger, Stephen Kepnes, Susan Shapiro, Alan Jay Richards, and Charles Winquist. I also renewed my acquaintance with Charles Long, who had come to Syracuse University directly from the University of North Carolina at Chapel Hill. This new group of friends offered inspiration and support at every turn. However, it was my trip to Auschwitz in the summer of 1991 that gave this book

---

[1] This appeared in *Echoes from the Holocaust*. The two other papers mentioned in the text are "Jews, Blacks, and Group Autonomy," *Social Theory and Practice* 14 (1988), and "American Slavery and the Holocaust: Their Ideologies Compared," *Public Affairs Quarterly* 5 (1991): 191–210. Reprinted with revisions in David Theo Goldberg and David Krausz (eds.), *Jewish Identity* (Philadelphia: Temple University Press, 1993).

its final form. No doubt I would have made the trip at some point, anyway, but Kepnes was the catalyst for my doing so at that time rather than later. I suspect that my reading Berl Lang's book, *Act and Idea in Nazi Genocide* (Chicago: University of Chicago Press, 1990), and writing a review of it[2] made me receptive to Kepnes's idea. My only regret is that he and I did not make the trip together as was originally planned. The review essay was written at the suggestion of Alan Berger, who has been a constant source of support and encouragement throughout the writing of this book. Both he and Kepnes have been boundless in their faith in me.

Before I left for Poland, Howard McGary and Bill Lawson sent me a copy of their manuscript *Between Slavery and Freedom* (Bloomington: Indiana University Press, 1992). My working through their magnificent manuscript energized me and gave my own thoughts greater focus. What is more, their sustained support and friendship over the better part of my professional career has meant much to me.

Although I began this work with fear and trembling, my surprise has been the support that I have received from so many quarters. Judith Jarvis Thomson offered a most instructive set of comments upon Chapter 3; Harold Brackman commented extensively upon Chapters 6 and 7; and Hilary Putnam gave me very good advice about Chapter 9. Thomas E. Hill, Jr., my friend and former colleague at the University of North Carolina at Chapel Hill, wrote extensive comments upon the first three chapters. Bernard Boxill also commented at length upon those chapters. For his friendship and support over the better part of my professional career, I am very grateful. Michael Pritchard wrote a great many comments upon the first five chapters. He has been a constant source of support since my days as a graduate student.

[2] "Characterizing and responding to Nazi Genocide: A Review Essay," *Modern Judaism* 11 (1991).

David Blumenfeld deserves special mention. He read the entire manuscript and commented extensively upon each chapter in the way that a good friend does. He did not merely criticize my arguments but made invaluable suggestions, often helping me to say better what I wanted to say. My long-time friend Jennifer Parkhurst, a developmental psychologist, not only offered many written comments but was also a part of this project from the beginning. That is, there is hardly an idea in this book that I have not tried out on her in some form or another. The intellectual acuity that she has brought to our conversations over the years is treasured beyond words.

I am also grateful for my instructive conversations with Aaron Ben-Zeev while visiting Israel on two occasions and with Jonathan Glover in Finland. While I rarely run into Amelie Rorty in New England, where she resides, our paths have crossed at most propitious moments in Israel, Finland, and California. Conversations with her on these occasions have been the single greatest influence upon the account of evil developed in Chapter 4. But for her, the account would have had a rather bizarre theological status.

I want also to mention Richard Wilkens, Simon Saks, Stephen Friedman, Henry Louis Gates, Julius Lester, Patricia Evans, Jamie Kalven, Henry Finder, Andrew Kerr, Michele Moody-Adams, Haim Rougemont, Clark Gilpin, Julian Weurth, and Alan Iser. Each has made a difference.

I want also to mention the influence of the course "American Slavery and the Holocaust," which I taught at the University of Chicago during the winter quarter of 1991. Jeffrey Smith and Shawn Watts were members of that class. Both challenged me and inspired me. The numerous conversations that Watts and I had were pivotal as my ideas for Part I of this book were taking form. I owe more to conversations with him than he might ever be inclined to realize. Jeffrey Cohen and Joshua Rosen, here at Syracuse University, did an independent study with me in the fall of 1992. Discussions with them played a most important role in the final formation of Chapter 5. After Cohen graduated, Rosen continued to work with me. He was a reader for the American Slavery and Holocaust course that I taught at Syracuse University in the spring of 1993, and he helped me to incorporate further refinements, resulting from class discussions, in the copyedited version of the manuscript. Throughout the final stages, he has been a godsend. I want to thank the Syracuse University students who enrolled in the American Slavery and the Holocaust course during the spring of 1993 for challenging me at numerous junctures along the way. A number of extremely important modifications were made as I endeavored to meet their challenges.

Finally, in this vein, I want to mention a few others, including Michael Stocker and Elizabeth Hegeman. Stocker, my colleague, did not read any of the manuscript. But I know he would have had I given it to him. Still, so many ideas in this book have been tried out on him that his voice is there. My confidence in myself that I could write this book has much to do with his unflagging support both spiritually and intellectually. I am grateful to Hegeman for many conversations about multiple personality disorders, for her marvelous command of and guidance through the literature on the subject. I thank Jane Cullen, Senior Acquisitions Editor at Temple University Press. It was her steadfast support and encouragement that got me through *Living Morally* (Philadelphia: Temple University Press, 1989). The same holds true for this book. If there is a Platonic form for editors, Cullen is surely an instantiation of it. Last but not least, I want to mention Annette Baier and Kurt Baier. The textured affirmation that I have received from both has constituted a wall of support, making it possible for me to pursue *my* philosophical interests.[3]

[3]See my "Moral Flourishing in an Unjust World," *Journal of Moral Education* 22 (1993), for an account of textured affirmation, which, as I have developed it, entails a display of confidence in an individual.

Thanks are also owed to the institutional support of Syracuse University, especially the chair of the Philosophy Department, Stewart Thau.

On a somewhat more personal note, I want first to mention Rabbi Shimon Brand, who from my days at Oberlin College has been a most instructive friend and colleague. To him this book is dedicated. Second, I want to mention three families: Norman and Joan Poltensen, Beverly and Bruce Marmor, and Arlene Kantor and Stephen Kepnes. They have all been sustaining. They are a part of the fabric of my life.

Much of this book was actually entered into a computer in its present form during jaunts to Puteaux (France), a town located at La Défense, just outside Paris—the perfect location for me. There Frederic and Joya Kiehl and their son Jean-Claude Kiehl gave me the use of their home during their absence. Without the solitude, often in the midst of a sea of people at La Défense, I could never have written this book. Jean-Claude and I became fast friends when we were undergraduate roommates. From the day he and I met, his parents have been wonderfully kind to me. I missed the parents tremendously when they returned from Maryland in the late 1970s to live in Paris, never imagining that one day their returning would play a pivotal role in my professional endeavors. In Paris proper, at the restaurant La Gazette, I had many dinner discussions of this book, thanks to the patience of the owners.

For sustained intellectual and spiritual support for more than a decade, for a friendship that has truly stood the test of time, I thank David Weissbord Sanford.

Miriam Lupeter Dobson, that "ole-fashioned" Jamaican woman who never allowed me to wallow in the valley of despair, and to whom I dedicated *Living Morally*, is now in a nursing home, having suffered a stroke that paralyzed her and severely impaired her speech. But her voice continues to be audible in my life—nay, it yet propels me forward.

I am well aware that there is much more to be said about the experiences of blacks and Jews. Another person might very well have written volumes of books to my one. But I shall be most grateful if this work constitutes a small beginning to an important dialogue that has not yet taken place. I do know, in any case, that there would not have been any book at all were it not for the good will and support of so many people—some named here, some not. The accumulative effect has been a veritable tidal wave of affirmation. THANK YOU.

Syracuse, New York
November 1992

PART I

On Becoming an Evil Self

Two Faces of Evil:
An Introduction

This is a study in evil. If wide-ranging diversity is the mark of humanity, then perhaps the price that is to be paid for such diversity is the capacity for evil itself. For in the name of difference, numerous atrocities have been committed. In this book, only two of these will be discussed: American Slavery and the Holocaust (which I will not always list in the order of temporal occurrence, as I have just done). A person with a quite different set of moral sensibilities might very well choose to focus on the atrocities that were committed by the Turks against the Armenians or by the Germans against the Poles or by Christian whites against either Native Americans or South Americans. And that person's moral sensibilities would not be more or less commendable simply on account of discussing a different set of atrocities.

Probably no one person could adequately depict all the moral horrors that have been visited upon the different peoples of the world. And to suppose that one could do so would, in many instances, be to make a mockery of the overwhelming moral pain that others have suffered. A person who focuses upon the moral suffering of some, and not others, does no one an injustice if that person is sufficiently mindful that the suffering of those about whom she or he writes does not even begin to exhaust the topic of suffering and if, in any case, the writer's aim is not one of invidious comparisons, as if a people cannot be said truly to have suffered unless they have suffered more than some or all others. Respectfully, but without apology, this book is an examination of but some of the sufferings of two groups of people, Jews and blacks. What follows first is a sketch of how I shall proceed. Then I offer a number of prefatory remarks concerning how this study is to be understood and the motivation for undertaking it. A natural worry is whether this work is replete with invidious comparisons. It is not. Indeed, absolutely nothing could be further from my aims, as I hope my prefatory remarks will make abundantly clear.

Rather than immediately taking up either the Holocaust or American Slavery, Part I is a general discussion of the nature of evil and some of the factors that make it possible. I shall discuss the matter first on an individual basis and then on a societal basis. My aim is a very limited one. I want to be able to make sense of evil without recourse to the view that human beings are naturally evil. Indeed, while there are those whose lives seem to be the very embodiment of evil—Nero and Adolf Hitler come readily to mind—it must be acknowledged that evil can be perpetrated by individuals who were once ordinary people, that is, morally decent people like you and me. Any satisfactory view of evil must make sense of this. Ordinary people, though open to moral criticism in many ways, would not imagine themselves participating in evil institutions. In fact, many ordinary people subscribe to values that are diametrically opposed to evil institutions. Alas, however, but for the compliance of enough ordinary people, some more compliant than others, neither the Holocaust nor American Slavery could have occurred. Nothing, including evil itself, occurs in a vacuum. Ordinary people, as I am now using the expression, invariably define the backdrop against which evil or, for that matter, good occurs.

In Part II, I focus specifically upon the differences between the Holocaust and American Slavery. My account will be at a very high level of generality, and will draw upon what is generally thought to be true about each evil institution. Some will find this gloss unnecessary because they hold that the truth about either will always be a matter of debate. I should like to think that at a very general level this is simply false. What is more, I am not concerned about persuading anyone of the occurrence of either institution. That I take as a given. Hence, this work does not speak to revisionists or provide grist for the mill of those who would like to silence them. There is simply no reason to think that any nonrevisionist historian of the Holocaust will ever deny that millions of Jews were gassed to death. There is no reason to think that any nonrevisionist historian of American Slavery will ever deny that black people were sometimes treated rather like so many cattle, worse than favorite pets. It is the traditional rendering of the evils of the Holocaust and American Slavery that I shall be drawing upon.

Needless to say, it can be debated to what extent, if any, either Jews or blacks were accomplices in their own suffering. I shall not enter into this debate. In either case, I should think it stunning if either none or most were collaborators. It is silly to be much disturbed by the complicity of some, as people have compromised themselves and their families with far less at stake.

A caveat: It has been rightly observed that Jews were not the only people killed during the Holocaust. Among other victims were Gypsies, Poles, and homosexuals, for example. If a complete account of the Holocaust must discuss everyone victimized, then I shall not be offering a complete account. Even a most cursory reading of Holocaust literature reveals that exterminating the Jews as Jews, rather than under some other description, was an absolutely central project of the Holocaust. If the extermination of others was equally central, it certainly took place under a different description. At the very least, then, this work focuses on one group the extermination of which was a central Holocaust project, namely the Jews.

In any study of the evil to which a people have been subjected, a most important question is: How has their past as victims of evil affected their future? This is the concern of Part III of this work, where I introduce the notions of group autonomy and historical narrative. Important differences between the ways that blacks and Jews have been affected by their past institutional sufferings are discussed here. Yet again it must be emphasized that an examination of these differences will not amount to a disingenuous way of claiming that either group has suffered more than the other. It is no doubt true that the extent of an evil institution must to some degree be measured by its effects upon the future of those upon whom it has been visited. But this consideration is by no means decisive. For if nothing else, it could be something of a miracle that a people has managed to survive an evil, in which case their survival alone could hardly be a measure of the magnitude of evil that they have suffered. Suffering may have been far worse than might be gathered from the fact that a group survived the horrors of an evil institution. That I intend to be absolutely even-handed in discussing the Holocaust and American Slavery is, I trust, indicated by my acceptance that both Jews and blacks have thought their survival somewhat miraculous. I dare say that Part III will be the most controversial of this work, if only because it is essentially interpretive. Just how either American Slavery or the Holocaust has affected its respective victims is not a matter of settled fact, at least not in all respects.

Between American Slavery and the Holocaust, there are those who would take it for granted that one was worse than the other. I do not. Nor is it a concern of mine to make such a case. There might be something objectionable about attempting such a determination, in any event. If one person has lost both legs and another has lost both arms, I should think it highly objectionable to attempt to determine who has been left the worse off. What is more, even allowing that such a determination could be made, it would surely be the wrong aspect with which to be concerned. And it would be hubris or self-pity of the worst sort for either to take any pride in the thought of having suffered the most, of having been left the worse off.

The Holocaust and American Slavery were profoundly evil in radically different ways, which immediately raises the question: Why write about both in the same work? Part of the answer, at any rate, is that the ways in which they differ are very illuminating. Our understanding of evil itself is deepened by looking at both without surreptitiously attempting to show that one was worse than the other. Notice, for example, that whereas the Holocaust (that is, the murdering of Jews in the camps) was shrouded in secrecy, nothing of the sort was true of American Slavery. Wherever the latter existed, it was very much a part of the public life. Yet, while the extermination of the Jews was state-mandated, slavery was not. Even when blacks were considered by the Constitution of the United States to be only three-fifths persons, slaveholding was not required of anyone. This is not to deny the strong social pressures that operated in favor of owning slaves, nor to minimize the significance of such social pressures. Still, poor whites in the South were not expected to own slaves; and in the matter of not owning slaves, rich whites in the North encountered far less social pressure than their Southern counterparts. By contrast, no group of people in Nazi Germany were, either officially or simply as a matter of social class, excluded from the state's endeavors to exterminate the Jews.

One more poignant contrast: The Nazi ideology toward Jewish children and Jewish adults was essentially the same. Both were to be eliminated. Jewish children, as such, were not to be given any special dispensation. By contrast, though being a child could never take away the inferiority of being a "nigger" and although slaveowners were often ruthless in their willingness to separate black children from their families, it remains true nonetheless that black children were often allowed to enjoy a measure of childhood and that black and white children were often allowed to play together. After all, a black child was not yet ready to assume fully the role of a slave; nor was the child a threat as such. Of course, there was no analogous adult role for Jews during the Holocaust that gave Jewish children a safety net.

From this consideration, or from the more general point that the aim of the Holocaust was to exterminate the Jews, whereas American Slavery did not seek the eradication of blacks, some will think it obvious that the Holocaust was a worse evil than American Slavery. This conclusion does not follow, however—not because wrongful death fails to be the ultimate form of harm that we take it to be, but because death is not the only ultimate form of harm that a person may endure. As one can imagine, I shall be saying more about this later.

Throughout this book, I shall offer a set of remarks that might be thought to imply that, overall, one of the two institutions under discussion was more evil than the other. But not so; I shall mean no such thing. Since the Holocaust and American Slavery were two radically different events, it should come as no surprise that some aspects of evil are to be found in one but not the other. Hence, it would be ludicrous to assume some overall ranking in terms of evil, simply on account of a difference between the two regarding some aspect of evil. I shall argue, for instance, that natal alienation was a deeply rooted feature of American Slavery and that the idea of the Jew as irredeemably evil was a deeply rooted feature of Nazi ideology. From these differences, in no way does it follow that one institution was worse than the other. Indeed, these differences are arguably incommensurable.

Thus, no significance should be attached to the order in which the two events are discussed or mentioned. As I have indicated, they were first mentioned in the order of their temporal occurrence. I shall follow that order only when temporal continuity of discussion requires it. Otherwise, the order in which they are mentioned will be random.

Let me straightaway speak to one form of invidious comparison, namely the comparison of numbers. This will amplify the warning made that, between American Slavery and the Holocaust, I do not mean to imply that one institution was more evil than the other.

I take it to be incontrovertible that the number of Jews who lost their lives owing to the Holocaust was six million or thereabouts. On the other hand, estimates of the number of blacks who lost their lives during the voyage from Africa to the United States—the Middle Passage, as it is traditionally called—have gotten wildly out of control.[1] Some have put the number as high as 200 million. This is incredible. Others have put the number as low as two million. Now just suppose, for the sake of argument, that the number of blacks who died during the Middle Passage and Slavery exceeded six million by several times. Would it inevitably follow from this that American Slavery was worse than the Holocaust? The answer is no. It would follow that the answer is yes only if the number of deaths were the only dimension of evil. But this is surely false, as seen in the phenomenon of extinction. The discussion of animals that follows is purely descriptive, in that no normative endorsement of any kind is implied.

If a species becomes extinct, that is a sad thing. It is, in fact, a travesty if the extinction is due to human destruction aimed at satisfying tastes in fashion only. The elephant is now threatened with extinction owing to the demand for ivory; the crocodile was once threatened with extinction owing to the demand for its skin. On the other hand, the number of tuna fish killed yearly to

[1]For a discussion of these matters, see Harold Brackman, *Farrakhan's Reign of Historical Error: The Truth Behind the Secret Relationship Between Blacks and Jews* (a Simon Wiesenthal Center Report, 1992), pp. 62–65.

satisfy human gastronomic tastes far exceeds the combined number of elephants and crocodiles killed each year, without the tuna fish being threatened with extinction. Likewise, no doubt, for salmon. The extinction of a species is not a function only of the number that die, but of whether the number of deaths (over one or more generations) seriously jeopardizes the species's ability to reproduce in sufficient numbers to insure its continued existence.

Not surprisingly, there is no absolute number that applies to all species in terms of extinction. Thus, although it may be wrong to kill 5,000 members of one species because doing so will bring it to the brink of extinction, it does not follow at all that, *for precisely the same reason*, it is wrong to kill 5,000 or even 20,000 members of a different species. By the same token, if one could kill 20,000 members of a given species without bringing it anywhere near the brink of extinction, that would hardly justify killing 20,000 members of a different species for which such a loss would guarantee extinction. As I have said, no normative endorsement is implied.

Lest there be any misunderstanding, I have not claimed, nor have I meant to claim, that the extinction or extermination of one group necessarily outweighs any numerical loss that another group may sustain.[2] The point is rather that extinction or extermination is of a different moral magnitude than numerical loss in and of itself.

The relevance of the preceding paragraphs to the numbers comparison between the Holocaust and American Slavery should be obvious. The horror stemming from the attempt to exterminate Group 1, when N number people were killed, is not equaled or exceeded in Group 2 simply because, and only because, $M + N$ number of people in Group 2 were killed, where M is several times greater than N. Extermination, like extinction,

---

[2] I am deeply grateful to conversations with Andrew Kerr that forced me to appreciate the need to make this point in the text.

is not tied to some absolute number. The number of a group remaining alive is crucial to whether a force has come close to exterminating a people. There are approximately thirty million blacks in the United States and approximately six million Jews. If a Hitler were to kill six million of each group, words could not begin to do justice to the magnitude of the difference between what the two groups had suffered.

Have I just implied that the Holocaust was worse than American Slavery? Absolutely not. What I said, in other words, was that if the same institution of evil is visited upon two different peoples simultaneously, all things being equal with the exception of the number of lives lost, then we do indeed have a basis for allowing loss of life to be an indication of the magnitude of the evil suffered. The Holocaust and American Slavery, however, are not various ways of referring to the same institution, but two entirely different evil institutions. Accordingly, the painful truth that the Holocaust posed a threat to the very existence of the Jewish people does not, thereby, make it worse than American Slavery. Nor, as we have just seen, does the greater number of deaths among blacks under American Slavery than among Jews in the Holocaust of itself warrant the conclusion that the former was worse than the latter.

Drawing upon the preceding discussion, I suggest the following as a most precise way of putting the difference between Slavery and the Holocaust: The very telos of Slavery was to bring about the utter dependence of blacks upon slaveowners. The very telos of the Holocaust was the extermination of the Jewish people. While each institution had other important aspects, I maintain that no account of either institution is satisfactory without the telos that I have attributed to it. Clearly, these two different characterizations of the telos point to radically different matrices for understanding the nature of the evil that was systemic of each institution. I dare say that this difference in the telos of each institution reveals at once that the number of deaths that resulted from each is not definitive of the evil of each institution. What is more, even if there were economic considerations that initally motivated both institutions—and there is simply no need to deny this—such considerations cannot be properly regarded as the telos of either institution.

Some final introductory comments. First, I should note that in some circles, it has become fashionable to use the term *holocaust* in reference to any objectionable practice of great magnitude: the Cambodian holocaust, the South African holocaust, and so on. Even the practice of abortion in the United States has been referred to as America's holocaust. I shall not follow this usage. First of all, I see nothing wrong with the convention of using a specific term to refer to a single set of practices, as *apartheid* is used to refer to oppression of blacks in South Africa and not to the oppression of other peoples in the world. Second, when a term has attained a certain currency in the language as a way of referring to a time of horror in a people's history, I think it is objectionable, downright disrespectful, to devalue that term by applying it indiscriminately to any horror one chooses. Throughout this work, I shall be using the term "Holocaust," capitalizing the first letter, to refer to but one historical event: the attempt by the Nazis to exterminate the Jews. On the other hand, I shall throughout write "American Slavery," capitalizing the first letters of both words; I shall likewise capitalize "Slavery" even when it is written alone, to make reference to American Slavery, though I shall not capitalize "slave(s)."

Second, while I intend to be even-handed in discussing American Slavery and the Holocaust, I shall not be concerned with the actual number of words devoted to each: say, 50,000 in one case and 34,500 in the other. Precisely because verbosity cannot possibly be a measure of profundity, equality of word-count is neither a necessary nor sufficient condition for moral even-handedness. At times, I shall have more to say about the Holocaust than about American Slavery. At other times, I shall have more to say about Slavery. The hope is that, in terms of enhancing our understanding of evil, the whole will be greater than the sum of its parts.

Third, throughout this work, especially in Part I, my aim is to gain some understanding as to how atrocities like American Slavery and the Holocaust could have occurred. I have no desire to excuse the participants in these two nefarious institutions. Here I am guided by the view that in the main these atrocities were committed by ordinary, morally decent human beings—people like you and me. No good comes from supposing that only those conceived in the very womb of evil could have so acted. To think in this way, as comforting as it might initially seem, fails to take seriously the fact that evil is often committed by those who earlier on in their lives rightly—or at least with some justification—considered themselves to be morally decent individuals. Any account of evil must be true to the reality that people of ordinary moral decency can be swept up by social tides, and that, as a result, people of ordinary moral decency can come to do what would hitherto have been unimaginable even in their own eyes. When this happens, it is the rare person who has such extraordinary resolve that she or he can then refrain from doing what is morally wrong.

Fortunately, however, extraordinary resolve is generally not necessary in order to stay clear of the social tides of evil. As Aristotle clearly and rightly saw: We are morally responsible for the wrong that we do, not so much because at the time of our actions we are capable of acting differently, but because at an earlier point we were capable of acting differently, and so need not have put ourselves in the position of ineluctably performing the wrong that we do. American Slavery and the Holocaust are not exceptions to this moral insight.

In this work, I aim to articulate the conceptual differences between the Holocaust and American Slavery rather than to compare the atrocities of one with the other.

The Human Condition

1. *Good and Bad*

Many suppose that human beings are naturally evil. By this it is meant that human beings are, at best, indifferent to the suffering they cause other humans and, at worst, they delight in such suffering—they find the suffering they cause others naturally satisfying. For some this view of naturalness is grounded in human biology. More particularly, aggression is said to serve the survival of the species. And it is deemed to be a rather small and obvious step from innate aggression to evil behavior. For others, the naturalness of evil is to be explained by way of the Judeo-Christian theological concept of original sin. In either case, however, if human beings are naturally evil, and if the impulse to do evil is deemed to be great enough, then the occurrence of evil itself hardly cries out for an explanation. The occurrence of such moral atrocities as the Holocaust and American Slavery, then, should not astound and bewilder us. On the contrary, the surprise should be that there have been comparatively few events of this kind in the history of humanity. That we have been relatively successful in keeping the impulse to do evil in check is what should surprise us. To be sure, it is conceded by all that

American Slavery and the Holocaust constitute extreme forms of evil. Still, on the supposition that human beings are naturally evil, the occurrence of these events does not seem to require much of an explanation.

As an explanation for evil, I shall not touch the topic of original sin. And while I accept the view that human beings have an innate capacity for aggression, I deny that it follows that human beings are naturally evil. Whatever else is true, the capacity for aggression is not tantamount to, nor does it entail, the capacity for evil. After all, we suppose that animals are capable of aggression; yet, notwithstanding all the anthropomorphizing that we do, we are not in the least bit inclined to think that animal aggression is the equivalent of evil behavior on their part. It may very well be that the willingness to engage in self-defense is made possible by the capacity for aggression. It may very well be that anger and rage would not be possible without the capacity for aggression. And it may certainly be true that without this capacity, much evil human behavior would not take place. Just the same, from none of this does it follow that human beings are, by nature, given to evil acts and that the good that humans do is a function of the extent to which aggression can be held in check.

There is an alternative. I shall refer to it as the fragility–goodness conception of human beings. In this view, human beings are not generally disposed to perform great self-sacrifices on behalf of strangers, nor are humans generally disposed to harm others. On the contrary, they are naturally moved by the weal and woe of others, and they want to eliminate suffering. The problem, however, is that human beings are especially fragile. A creature is fragile if things can easily prevent its natural propensities from being realized or can readily frustrate their operation. Although not all things of high quality are fragile, there is no incompatibility between fragility and excellence of quality. Indeed, in some instances there is a positive correlation between the two. Dishes of fine china, for example, are extremely fragile. Silk is a finer yet more delicate material than cotton. Exquisite foods require far more careful preparation and precise cooking. So, too, it is with human beings, as the case of child development makes abundantly clear.

In terms of the well-being and flourishing of the child, the parent-child relationship, for instance, is a paradigm of a fragile relationship among human beings. Something like the following is true with regard to the proper parent-child relationship. Parents should love their child, and in turn the child should come to love them. Parents should guide and direct their child but not be overbearing. Notwithstanding the child's occasional failures, parental love should always be forthcoming; and the child should always feel that this is so. Love should be forthcoming even when praise should not be. Thus, the child should feel loved even in the face of parental chastisement. The child should never be made to feel that it is simply an extension of the will of its parents, or that it will be rejected by them because they disapprove of its behavior.

Needless to say, there are a multitude of ways in which things can go wrong in the parent-child relationship. Regrettably, things can go wrong even when parents have quite good intentions and mean to do right by their child. Thus, parents overly concerned that their child not go astray may raise the child with an iron hand and be overprotective, with the result that they stifle the spontaneous and exploratory behavior essential to a child's self-discovery. Or, parents may mistakenly think that their child will feel loved by them only if they are uncritical of any of its behavior, with the result that the child has a narcissistic view of itself and is unable to accept constructive criticism from others. Or, notwithstanding the admirable behavior of its parents, the child may have an untoward experience that puts it beyond the the salubrious effect of parental love and support.

Unsuspected sexual abuse from a revered member of the family—such as a grandfather—would be an example of this. Family members, neighbors, visitors—just about anyone who meets grandfather—all think that he is simply wonderful, every child's dream. Indeed, children flock to him. So a charge of sexual abuse would not merely fall on deaf ears but would in fact be greeted with great hostility.

We see the fragility of the parent-child relationship because we see that things can go quite wrong even among the most well-meaning of parents. But its fragility is greater still because parents themselves often turn out to be considerably less than well-meaning in raising their child. Owing perhaps to their own bad experiences as youngsters, some parents mentally and physically abuse their child; others put the wants of adult relationships substantially above the needs of the child. There are parents who simply should not be parents; they lack the emotional stability that good parenting requires.

Although many things can and often do go wrong, the proper parent-child relationship remains one in which parental love contributes to the well-being and flourishing of the child. The parent-child relationship with regard to the well-being of the child is fragile precisely because there are so many ways in which its proper realization may be prevented. The existence of obstacles does not in any way count against the truth that there is a proper way for things to go in the parent-child relationship with regard to the child.

The parent-child relationship is not only an excellent example of fragility; as it is used here, the example also gives us some insight into why human beings are fragile with respect to the realization of modest moral good. According to the modest fragility–goodness conception, human beings do not take delight in causing others harm. But this is not true in every case, any more than it is true that a child's well-being is secured, come what may. As is well is known, there is a significant correlation between being a victim of sexual abuse and being guilty of committing sexual abuse.

According to the fragility model of human goodness, things are as they should be when human beings have certain sensibilities that make the suffering of others repulsive and, a fortiori, the suffering of others at their own hand repulsive. That conception does not entail, however, that those sensibilities will be in place no matter what happens. Those sensibilities can be prevented from developing or can be deadened by a myriad of things.

We are not faced with having to choose between the dichotomy of human beings as naturally evil, on the one hand, or naturally saintly, on the other. The latter can be understood to mean that, at the very least, human beings are naturally altruistic in their orientation, sufficiently so that they delight in making sacrifices—often substantial ones—on behalf of others. This is what I call the ideal conception of human goodness.

In contrast, we have the modest conception of human goodness. Under this conception, while human beings are not naturally altruistic in the sense just delineated, they do not, on the other hand, delight in causing of the suffering of others. Moreover, in this view, far from being indifferent to the suffering of others, human beings very strongly prefer not to play a role in such suffering; and to learn that they have done so disturbs them greatly. So, though it is true, according to this conception, that human beings fall considerably short of the ideal conception of human goodness sketched in the preceding paragraph, it is equally true that human beings fall considerably short of being naturally disposed to commit acts of evil against one another. This book presupposes the modest conception of human goodness as the backdrop against which the fragility model of human goodness is to be understood.

I believe that the fragility–goodness model gives us a more

natural way of understanding evils that occur in the world without resorting to the thesis that human beings are innately evil. The model is capable of explaining the evil that occurs in human life without appealing to the very strong thesis that human beings are innately evil; hence, the model renders that very strong thesis otiose. Of course, no doubt some individuals are rightly regarded as innately evil. The model does not deny that; it merely insists that nothing is gained by regarding all human beings in that way.

The fragility–goodness model yields a rhetorical victory as well. We often regard the occurrence of human suffering at the hands of others as tragic. That such suffering is tragic turns out to be considerably more true given the fragility–goodness model of human beings than it does given the view that they are inherently evil. Under the former concept it can be said that the evil might very well not have occurred had things not gone wrong in the lives of the individuals involved, whereas this line of reasoning makes very little sense if, to begin with, we suppose that human beings are innately evil.

It might be objected that the fragility–goodness model of human development comes too close for comfort to absolving human beings of moral responsibility for most of the evil that they do. First of all, it should be noted that, even if this is so, the idea that human beings are naturally evil is no less open to this objection. Second, it is significant that even if both models are open to this criticism, there are very strong reasons for preferring the fragility–goodness model to the innate-evil model. I shall offer these reasons shortly. Owing to the following considerations, however, I doubt that either model is open to the criticism that it entirely absolves human beings of moral responsibility.

Observe that the fact of being innate does not determine how a trait manifests itself.[1] And it is possible that a person can be

---

[1] I am deeply indebted here to Patricia S. Greenspan, "Unfreedom and Responsibility," in Ferdinand Schoeman (ed.), *Responsibility, Character, and the*

blamed for how an innate trait manifests itself even if the person cannot be blamed for the fact that it does manifest itself. For instance, if a congenital disease is exacerbated by alcohol consumption, then the person who imbibes can be blamed for aggravating the condition, but not for having the disease in the first place. The model of innate evil would entirely absolve persons of moral responsibility only if the model entailed that persons have no control over the way in which evil or undesirable traits manifest themselves. But the model entails no such thing. A person born with aggressive tendencies, for instance, might avoid activities that trigger aggressive behavior. He might avoid certain kinds of bar scenes. He might avoid seeing certain kinds of films unless doing so is part of a social evening with friends, when the film is followed by a meal and conversation. He would be blameworthy for failing to do these things, though not for the aggressive disposition itself.

Clearly, if the model of innate evil does not settle the question of how evil traits will be manifested, then a fortiori neither does the fragility–goodness model. I noted that there is a significant correlation between victimization through sexual abuse and the commission of sexual abuse. No one who has been a victim of such abuse must inevitably perpetrate that horror upon others, even if it is true that persons who have been abused are, for various psychological reasons, more prone to prey on others than those who have not been abused. Victims of sexual abuse can take steps to insure that they do not treat others in a like manner. While the fragility–goodness model allows for many deficits with respect to achieving moral behavior, it does not entail that those deficits cannot be dealt with successfully.

To be sure, none of this achievement is easy. Indeed, we might very well be more understanding of sexually abusive be-

---

Emotions: New Essays in Moral Psychology (New York: Cambridge University Press, 1987).

havior on the part of victims of sexual abuse than on the part of
those who do not have such a past. However, the point of the
remarks in the preceding few paragraphs has not been to show
that it is easy to overcome traits or psychological histories that
make a person prone to engage in detrimental behavior towards
others, but only to point out that the existence of such traits or
psychological profiles does not make detrimental behavior inevitable. Hence, their existence does not entirely absolve a person
of moral responsibility.

There are several reasons for believing that the fragility–goodness model is superior to the innate-evil model. While the former model entails that much needs to be in place if humans are
modestly good, the model does not in principle rule out the
realization of modest goodness. The model claims only that this
state of affairs can be difficult to realize. Further, the fragility–
goodness model allows that the realization of modest goodness
can yield a stable state of affairs. That is, if modest goodness
were realized in enough lives, it would generate its own support,
and the untoward effects of wrongdoing would be minimal.[2]

With the innate-evil model, by contrast, neither point seems
to hold. (It will be recalled that I have put aside the theological
view of innate evil.) According to the innate model, the reason
why evil occurs has nothing to do with the things that go wrong
in human development; instead, evil is tied to aggression; and, if
Darwin is right, aggression is very much a natural feature of the
human condition. So in principle, it precludes the possibility
that persons will not desire to harm others. And while the model
is no doubt compatible with the idea that the desire to do evil
can be held in check, it would seem that the model is clearly
incompatible with stability along these lines—at least not without a story of deep, deep repression of desires. By contrast, the

[2] The account of the parent-child relationship extends the account I put forth
in *Living Morally* (Philadelphia: Temple University Press, 1989), chaps. 2 and 3.

fragility–goodness model requires no such story of repression; the model maintains not that the desire to harm others can be successfully held in check, but that if enough things go right, then the desire simply will not occur. If nothing else, then, it would certainly follow that stability is far more easily achieved on the fragility–goodness model than on the innate-evil model.

Here is a third reason. While there are many facets to evil, a most striking one is that intensely evil acts are sometimes committed by individuals who take themselves to have a morally decent character. Moreover, individuals who have committed such appalling acts are not judged by history itself to be evil, although the histories of their lives are written by people who abhor the practices in which these historical figures took part.

Thomas Jefferson springs to mind here. He was a brilliant and noble man. He was one of the architects of the Constitution of the United States. He was also a slaveholder. Yet certainly no one regards him as an evil man, although the practice of slavery, quite unlike some other forms of racism, is not something in which a person can unwittingly participate. Worse, Jefferson was explicitly aware of the moral problems that slavery involved. That is, whereas other slaveholders seemed to think it obvious that blacks should be slaves and gave the matter no further thought, Jefferson actually wrestled with the issue, writing some of the most eloquent antislavery remarks to be found, even as he owned slaves and took a black slave as his mistress.[3] The fra-

---

[3]In a letter to Henri Gregoire, Jefferson wrote: "Be assured that no person living wishes more sincerely than I do, to see a complete refutation of the doubts I have myself entertained and expressed on the grade of understanding allotted to them [Negroes] by nature, and to find that in this respect they are on a par with ourselves. My doubts were the result of personal observation on the limited sphere of my own State, where the opportunities for the development of their genius were not favorable, and those of exercising it still less so." In a letter to James Heaton, Jefferson wrote: "The revolution in public opinion which this cause [the ending of slavery] requires, is not to be expected in a day, or perhaps in an age; but time, which outlives all things, will outlive this evil also. My

gility–goodness model offers a better explanation of persons like Jefferson than does the innate-evil model.

For one thing, it acknowledges a particularly interesting aspect of human fragility, namely that relentless consistency is not an attribute of human beings. Human beings are capable of remarkable insularity in their lives with respect to their beliefs. It is well known that most people have beliefs the logical implications of which would entail that they act in ways other than they do. For example, individuals may believe that their incomes suffice for their needs several times over and that it is wrong for so many others to have to do without basic necessities; yet—except for a few modest acts of charity—they enjoy their incomes to the fullest. To take a more specific example, it is possible for a talented Jewish woman to oppose sexism strongly and to take numerous stands against it in the workplace, and yet attend an Orthodox synagogue where she puts up with male privilege to an extent that would be unthinkable to her in any other context. There are often incommensurable fundamental values in life, and people choose not to choose between them. No self-deception need be involved.

A related consideration here has to do with the issue of choice itself. Although choice and autonomy are highly regarded in the Western tradition, it is simply false that all significant features of the self are chosen. Though neither our ethnicity nor our gender is chosen, they are hardly insignificant aspects of our lives. It is

---

sentiments have been forty years before the public. . . . Although I shall not live to see them consummated, they will not die with me; but living or dying, they will ever be in my most fervent prayer." Both quotes are from *Thomas Jefferson: Writings*, ed. Merrill D. Peterson (New York: Library of America, 1984). Jefferson freed five of his slaves in his will. See under "Chronology," date 1826. See also John W. Blassingame's *Slave Testimony: Two Centuries of Letters, Speeches, Interviews, and Autobiographies* (Baton Rouge: Louisiana State University Press, 1977), and his *The Slave Community: Plantation Life in the Antebellum South*, 2d. ed. (New York: Oxford University Press, 1979).

equally true that many of the fundamental values of life are not a matter of choice. To be sure, values are more easily changed than ethnicity and gender. But this truth should not blind us to the fact that values can nonetheless be extremely intransigent. A person who has one set of values can adopt another set inconsistent with the first but find that it is impossible to give up the first set—indeed, that there are good reasons for not doing so.

Thus, in the previous example, the talented Jewish woman may be deeply committed to the preservation of Jewish culture and believe that, given present social conditions, Orthodox Judaism is indispensable to this end. She did not choose to be a Jew. When she later came to have deep feminist values, she was unwilling to choose between feminism and her religious traditions. And while it is true that she chose to be a feminist, it may very well be that the catalyst for her choice was the date-rape of her roommate in college and the silence on the part of college officials that accompanied it, none of which was owing to choices on her part.

The point here is that a person can come to have incommensurable values without choosing to be in a situation where one set of values conflicts with another. In her choosing to be a feminist, we need not suppose that the woman in our example had the intention of acquiring a set of values that would conflict with the traditions of Judaism as she interpreted them. Although she in fact acquired such a set of values—and we may even suppose that she acquired those values intentionally—we are not logically forced to conclude that she intentionally chose to have the conflicting values in question, owing to the opacity of reference here.[4] Of course, intentional choice should not be confused with

---

[4]This follows from what is known in philosophy as the opacity of reference with respect to intentions. If (1) Gomez intentionally chooses B and (2) B entails C or is even identical to C, it does not follow that Gomez intentionally chooses C, if only because Gomez need not know that condition 2 is true. Recall the survey of men who thought it not wrong for a man to intend to have sex

the issue of moral responsibility. Even if a person did not in fact choose for something to occur, the person may be morally responsible for that occurrence.

It is a part of the fragility of human beings, then, that they can come to have conflicting values about which they are not self-deceived, without ever choosing to have the conflict between those values.

A corollary, if you will, to this view is that human beings are capable of compartmentalizing. Let us say that a person is compartmentalizing if he regularly engages in a mode of behavior without regard to the important ways in which that behavior bears upon another significant aspect of his life. There are degrees of compartmentalization, of course, and the truth of the matter is that most individuals engage in some form of minimal compartmentalization all the time, for it is a coping mechanism among human beings. It prevents a kind of reality overload. The decision not to worry about something, in the common vernacular, can often be a form of compartmentalization. To be sure, a person can worry needlessly. But it is also possible not to be mindful of things to which one really ought to pay attention.

Nowadays, in a world of AIDS, the adult who engages in unprotected sexual intercourse is engaging in compartmentalizing. Compartmentalizing often occurs because values or goals have a very deep hold on us, yet the consequences of realizing them are anything but favorable. Ideally, we should give up values or goals the attainment of which has an adverse effect upon our lives. But this is easier said than done. Society itself often makes that difficult to do. For example, being sexually active or at least

---

with a woman by force but who agreed that it was wrong for a man to rape a woman, though rape is generally defined as having sexual intercourse by force. In fact, we can have opacity of reference even if we have all the relevant knowledge about a situation. If Gomez wants to marry Jones and Jones is an alcoholic, it does not follow that Gomez wants to marry an alcoholic, as if Gomez were looking for that characteristic in a marriage partner.

sexually desirable is held up as a good in many quarters of society, and to such an extent, that few have any chance of remaining inured to this end as a good for them to attain. What is more, so much is made of spontaneity, of yielding to raw passion, that often enough a person who gives much thought to the consequences of such matters is made to appear all but prudish. Not surprisingly, then, people go right on having unprotected sex notwithstanding the well-known deleterious consequences of doing so. I am referring not only to AIDS, but also to the birth of unwanted children, which in this day is less likely to be for the better. This is compartmentalization. It is not owing to mental illness or to some defect in reasoning; rather, it is a way of coping with two very disparate worlds, one being the world of advertisements, television, and movies, in which the good life revolves around giving in to the moment of sexual desire, the other being the harsh world of reality, where giving in to such moments can often have disastrous consequences.

As I have explicated it, the capacity to compartmentalize is not necessarily a human failing. It is one of the psychological mechanisms that enable human beings to cope with wrongs that they must systematically endure (as we shall see in Chapter 5), but just as it serves a useful purpose, it can serve an evil purpose as well. That is very much a feature of the fragility of humanity.

2. *Immoral Rapprochement*

A person might agree that values need not be a matter of choice but insist that a person's actions must be. I wish not so much to deny this as to draw attention to the obliging interpersonal historical context of actions. One reason why most of us can easily pass by a beggar on the street, even as we head off to dine at a fine restaurant, spending more money on a meal than can possibly be justified in terms of nutritional value, is that we have no obliging interpersonal historical context with that person. For instance, we have no debts of gratitude to the beggar, and there is nothing that we want from him. Nor is there any sense in which any past actions on our part have given this unfortunate any sort of claim on us. It is not as if a week ago we said to the beggar, "Look, I do not have any additional money now. But I may come here next week and if you are here, then perhaps—just perhaps—I will have some change for you." If we had said this, a great many of us would feel a little obliged to give the beggar something this week, thinking that our previous remarks had given him a reason for expecting something from us, although we had hardly promised anything. We had not even promised to return. To be sure, it is our choice whether to give him the money. However, it is a choice that is not without an obliging interpersonal historical context. Without in any way raising the specter of determinism, what we said last week to the beggar is quite relevant to what we decide to do when we encounter the beggar this time.

A great many of our actions can be understood in this way. They are hardly determined, but an obliging interpersonal historical context, or some aspect thereof, plays a quite relevant role in what we decide to do. An initial response to a beggar on the street is the closest that many of our actions come to occurring in a social vacuum. It goes without saying that obliging interpersonal historical contexts may differ in both force and form. Our decision to deny the same request to one acquaintance but not another can very often be explained by none other than a difference in force between the two obliging interpersonal historical contexts. And as the example of the beggar makes clear, in such a historical context, people may do what they would not otherwise have done.

The following is a more textured example of an obliging interpersonal context that differs in both force and form from that of the beggar. The force is owing to gratitude rather than to a previous commitment or commitment-like set of remarks.[5]

Suppose that General Sanchez, a person of admirable moral character, discovers that an officer who has an otherwise spectacular record plagiarized an entrance examination that he took ten years ago for the highly regarded Submarine Academy. In one scenario, the officer turns out to be Jones, a complete stranger to Sanchez; in another scenario, the officer is Smith, a long-time family friend who on many occasions has endured ostracism and threats, even a few instances of physical abuse, because of his deep ties with an Hispanic family. By making the plagiarism public, Sanchez can ruin the career of the officer. On the other hand, Sanchez may quietly overlook the event, knowing full well that if he does, the matter will never arise again. I have not filled out Sanchez's character enough to allow for a reasonable guess as to how he might behave. And I shall not. Sanchez may be the kind of person who would make the matter public no matter what. I want only to point out, though, that if Sanchez should make the plagiarism public in Jones's case but not in Smith's case, the differences in obliging interpersonal historical contexts would make Sanchez's behavior perfectly understandable to a great many people, although it is undeniable that Sanchez would be overlooking a significant moral wrong.

The force of this example, clearly, is that, assuming that neither Sanchez nor Smith is evil, we can think it most understandable that one person overlooks a significant moral wrong done by another. After all, ten years have passed and the officer has an otherwise exemplary record. Then there is the fact that the officer is Smith. Even if the officer were Jones, some would none-

[5]For a discussion of the topic of gratitude, see Lawrence C. Becker, *Reciprocity* (New York: Routledge and Kegan Paul, 1986); Claudia Card, "Gratitude and Obligation," *American Philosophical Quarterly* 25 (1988); Terrance McConnell, *Gratitude* (Philadelphia: Temple University Press, 1993), ch. 7.

theless think Sanchez cruel for making the plagiarism public. But Smith makes it especially difficult for Sanchez to avoid that charge, regardless of how firmly Sanchez's feet may be planted in the soil of moral rectitude. Need anyone be reminded that forgiveness and compassion are virtues?

Although we may suppose that it was Sanchez's choice not to make Smith's plagiarism public, Sanchez hardly chose to be in the predicament of having to decide whether or not to do so. And although Sanchez would readily acknowledge the obliging aspects of his relationship with Smith, it would never have occurred to Sanchez that the obliging interpersonal history between him and Smith would one day result in his overlooking a significant moral wrong on Smith's part. It is possible for a person to be faced with choosing to overlook another's wrongdoing, even to feel considerable pull toward doing so, without in any way being morally responsible for being in that predicament. Nor need it be a morally corrupt character that explains why a person feels considerable pull toward overlooking a wrongdoing. In overlooking Smith's past wrong, it may be that Sanchez himself commits a wrong today. If so, nothing I have said entails that Sanchez is neither morally responsible nor morally blameworthy for what he does, which brings me to the final point I want to make about the Sanchez scenario.

There is a tradition in moral philosophy deeply influenced by both Plato and Kant according to which a rational person is one who does not knowingly do what is wrong, insofar as reasoning is operating in that person's life as it ought to be. No doubt many would argue that neither the Holocaust nor American Slavery would have occurred had reason been operating in the lives of individuals as it should have been. Perhaps. But the Sanchez story suggests that life is somewhat more complicated than that. If, indeed, Sanchez does what is wrong in overlooking Smith's wrongdoing, owing to the obliging interpersonal histories between them, it is not at all obvious, given the way that I have told the story, that Sanchez's wrongdoing is to be explained by the failure of reason to be operating in his life as it ought to be. I do not see how it can be demonstrated that Sanchez acts outside the realm of reason, whatever one might feel about his behavior. It can be quite plausibly held that he has acted ever so reasonably. If so, then there are times when it is possible for a person to feel that the weight of reason itself militates in favor of doing what is wrong. It is possible for a morally decent person to feel precisely this.

Recall the observation made earlier that a striking fact about acts of evil is that they are sometimes committed by those who regard themselves as morally honorable, and who are later judged by others to have been such, although these historical judges would in no way approve of the evil actions that were committed.

I should like to introduce the notion of an immoral rapprochement. Obviously, people choose every day between doing what is right and what is wrong. But some choices that we must make would seem to be forced upon us, as when we must respond to a personal request from a specific person or when it is our responsibility to make certain decisions. Or, it may be simply that we are confronted with non-normal moral circumstances that immediately require that we act one way or the other. Let me assume that the idea of a forced choice is intuitive enough, except to say that the class of forced choices that I am interested in do not arise out of prior wrongdoings on a person's part. A person who accidentally kills someone in the course of committing a burglary must now make a forced choice regarding the dead body. This is a culpable forced choice. Here, I am interested only in innocent forced choices. It goes without saying, though, that it can be a matter of debate whether a forced choice is culpable or innocent.

We have an immoral rapprochement, then, when a person is faced with an innocent forced choice of performing (or not performing) an immoral act and the person is moved to perform the immoral act owing not to a desire to do what is immoral but to considerations that may be morally neutral or even morally commendable—or, at any rate, they would be so in a different context. An obliging interpersonal historical context is a paradigm example of such a consideration. Fear can be another consideration of this sort, as can the deep desire to win the approval of a person (usually in a position of power or authority). And it goes without saying that considerations can operate in conjunction with one another. It may be that Roberts is tremendously eager to win the approval of Johnson, a long-time family friend who has bailed out the Robertses financially on a number of occasions. And no one can reasonably deny that out of fear a person may be moved to perform an immoral act that she would otherwise reject, without its being true in the least that she desired to do what is immoral. To be sure, the fear may be irrational. But irrational fear is no less real on that account, as in the case of phobias, which can be crippling. In the story of Sanchez, we have an example of gratitude operating in this way. Compassion also comes to mind, as do feelings of affection. A person may seem to display such contrition for a wrong that one has compassion on him rather than charge him as the duty of one's office unequivocally requires.

Clearly, some people do what is wrong deliberately. I have not denied that. Others succumb to temptation because the wrong in question holds too great an attraction. I have not denied that. However, these ways of doing what is wrong do not exhaust the moral landscape. I believe that we must allow that a person can be moved to do what is wrong out of morally commendable considerations or on account of factors that do not bespeak a weakness of character. The idea of immoral rapprochement is meant to capture this reality. It does not deny that a wrong has been done. Nor does it deny that the doer should be reproached or blamed. It insists only that, as an explanation for why the person did the wrong, we need not suppose morally reprehensible motives. To be sure, a person may be criticized for letting honorable motives get in the way of doing what is right, but that is another matter entirely.

When the idea of immoral rapprochement is seen as part of the fragility–goodness model of human beings, this model clearly yields far greater insight into the human condition than does the innate-evil model of human beings. This latter model insists that the very idea of genuinely morally decent people is nothing but a useful fiction at best. Our wonderment that morally decent people sometimes do what is wrong is thus dismissed as misguided in the first place. The extended fragility–goodness model, far from simply ruling the wonderment out of court, explains the wonderment by bringing out what it is about the human condition, anchored as it is in social relations, that sometimes results in morally decent people feeling strongly pulled to commit the wrong of overlooking another's wrongdoing. This is clearly vastly superior to making it an article of faith that people are innately evil and so will inevitably overlook wrongdoing from time to time. The fragility–goodness model allows us to have it both ways, by explaining how we can start with genuinely morally decent individuals yet sometimes end up with wrongdoing; whereas the innate-evil model successfully explains wrongdoing only by ruling out the possibility of there being genuinely morally decent people. The simplicity of the innate-evil model comes at too high a price.

Before moving on, it is worth mentioning what may very well have occurred to the reader, namely that compartmentalization and obliging interpersonal historical contexts can operate together in quite unseemly ways. The Sanchez scenario was very limited: a matter of overlooking a single wrong act, not all that egregious, committed many years ago. But life is not always so nicely packaged. It is possible for an obliging interpersonal historical context to call for overlooking repeated performances of a far more serious wrong act. Suppose that at considerable risk to himself, Smith had saved not only Sanchez's life but the lives of Sanchez's two sons, four and six years of age. On any account, Sanchez owes Smith a considerable debt of gratitude. Sanchez then unwittingly discovers that Smith routinely accepts small bribes from rich suppliers; and Smith knows that Sanchez has stumbled upon this. Smith wastes no time in reminding Sanchez that he and his sons owe their lives to Smith. Understandably, Sanchez very much feels the pull of this, and he asks Smith to avoid him as much as possible and to make no reference to the matter. Unlike his reaction in our first case, Sanchez is compartmentalizing with respects to Smith's behavior. He does not want to be reminded that, by not going to the authorities, he is letting a person do what is morally wrong to others—that he is something of an accomplice in Smith's wrongdoing.

The irony here can hardly be lost on one. Indisputably, gratitude is a morally appropriate response to benevolence when the benefactor is known. Acts of benevolence that give rise to debts of gratitude (not all do, as with anonymous donations to charity) create what I have called an obliging interpersonal historical context. Such contexts can be exploited to serve morally objectionable ends. Hitler was a genius at this.

I want now to say a word about moral responsibility. I take it as a given that almost anyone who regards both the American Slavery and the Holocaust as profoundly evil institutions also believes that (most of) those who participated in these institutions not only did what is quite immoral but are rightly held morally responsible. This poignantly raises the issue of free will, and the problems associated with it: Moral responsibility is impossible in a world that is void of free will. The considerations are familiar enough; and I shall not rehearse them here. Nor do I have anything illuminating to say about the issue. I assume that there are no facts about either the Holocaust or American Slavery that force us to say that in the overwhelming majority of cases, the individuals performed the moral horrors they did without free will.

I believe that a deep virtue of the notion of an immoral rapprochement is that it allows that a person has acted freely in doing what is morally wrong, as it gives us insight into how the person could have felt the pull of the moral wrong. For as the notion has been developed, although this pull is far from trivial, it is not tantamount to a compulsion, psychological or otherwise, to perform the immoral act in question. In our previous examples, Sanchez cannot claim, with any plausibility, that he was compelled by the nature of his past relationship with Smith to overlook Smith's wrongdoing, though Sanchez can explain why he was deeply moved to act in this way. We can actually imagine Sanchez's claiming that he could not have lived with himself had he not overlooked Smith's wrongdoing. Yet, forceful as that claim is, we would not suppose that Sanchez meant that he lacked the freedom to report Smith. A pull, whether moral or immoral, is not a form of psychological compulsion.

3.   *Understanding Obedience to Authority*

Supplemented with the account of immoral rapprochement, the fragility–goodness model can be easily extended to the phenomenon of obedience to authority. I have argued that an obliging interpersonal context can be a very potent explanation for feeling strongly inclined to overlook a wrongdoing on the part of another. One of the most obliging interpersonal contexts for a great many human beings is that of respect for (legitimate) authority. This should come as no surprise; for we begin life quite incapable of caring for ourselves and properly interpreting our own experiences. Both our well-being and our self-understanding are inextricably tied to others. What I most want to draw attention to here is the poignant truth that respecting authority

implies trusting it to be right—indeed, yielding one's own views
of how one should behave in a given situation to authority's
dictates. This is obviously the case for the child with respect to
her or his parents, and to her or his teachers as well. A characteristic feature of legitimate authority, then, is that we allow that
it can be right, and so right to follow, in spite of our own assessment of matters. We are generally well disposed to adopt a submissive attitude toward authority that we accept as legitimate.
While it would be rewarding to think that with adulthood the
disposition to adopt a submissive attitude toward authority
passes away entirely, the evidence would seem to point in the
other direction. The reality that there are far fewer legitimate
authority figures in an adult's life is not evidence that adults are
not at all inclined to be submissive to authority.

In Western culture, of course, Socrates is generally held up as
the person that we should emulate in terms of our attitude toward authority: We should not be blindly accepting of any authority; moreover, we should have the moral wherewithal to
stand up to injustice wherever and whenever we find it, be it in
ourselves or others. When it comes to eschewing injustice and
embracing justice, no relationship is too precious to forgo; no
benefit is too great to refuse. To live otherwise is to live a moral
flaw. For human beings, this is impossible—or at least an extremely onerous demand.

Human beings are quintessentially social creatures. Not only
is their conception of themselves inescapably tied to others, but
precisely because this is so, human beings can be influenced by
others in morally untoward ways. The Socratic ideal assumes
that moral leverage surpasses all other forms of leverage in the
social arena, that persons need no greater assurance than that the
truth—the moral truth, in particular—is on their side. That is
not the case, for our moral self is but a part of who we are, of our
social self. Being loved, having friends, being physically attractive, having skills, and the like all have a social orbit that is rather

independent of morality. That is, their importance, like that of a variety of bodily functions such as eating and sleeping, is not tied to the ends of morality. No amount of intellectual posturing will make it so. Nor does the fact that these things weigh significantly with us independent of morality reveal a deep moral flaw.

It will be remembered that Socrates did not question what he believed to be legitimate and just authority. Recall that, although he was sentenced to death, Socrates at no time held that he was treated unjustly by the state, let alone that its authority was illegitimate. This is to be admired. Suffice it to say, however, that the life of Socrates cannot plausibly be regarded as defining reasonable expectations for other human beings—any more than the life of Mother Theresa can, though her life, too, is certainly one to be admired. Although a moral theory must allow for both moral heroes and moral saints, it cannot make the activities of such individuals definitive of moral decency.

For the average person, then, there is the presumption that legitimate authority is right. This is part of the social upbringing of most individuals. And the state, along with various academic and religious institutions, stands as one of the most salient forms of legitimate authority in a society, though each may differ in the hold it has upon our lives and in the range of its authority. When we ourselves do not have some standing in any of these institutions, it can be very difficult not to adopt a submissive attitude toward one who has status, especially in an institution that has a strong hold upon our lives. Thus, the official position of the Catholic Church on various issues—such as abortion, homosexuality, responsibility for the death of Christ—is of enormous influence precisely because of the very strong hold that the institution has on the lives of many.

It is in the light of the preceding remarks that we should understand Stanley Milgram's classic study, *Obedience to Authority*.[6]

[6]New York: Harper and Row, 1974. For another seminal discussion of obedience in wrongdoing, see Herbert C. Kelman and V. Lee Hamilton, *Crimes of Obedience* (New Haven: Yale University Press, 1989).

But first, a prefatory remark. Any account of the Milgram experiment that explains how so many ordinary, decent people ended up doing what was wrong, even after the wrong was abundantly clear to them, should not turn the participants into moral monsters-in-waiting. It should leave their moral decency intact—so much so that our own confidence that we would not have done likewise in their situation is at least somewhat shaken. Indeed, the story is a chilling one only if we have a bit of difficulty putting some distance between ourselves and the participants—unless, of course, there is a very special story to be told about our lives that would indicate that our lives far surpass the requirements of ordinary moral decency.

The stunning surprise of the experiment was that many participants thought to be morally decent individuals obeyed officials' orders to administer what the participants had been led to believe, for the sake of the experiment, were increasingly more potent electric shocks to the so-called subjects (in fact, people who knew the nature of the experiment). The participants continued to intensify the electric shocks although they could plainly see (that is: were led to believe) that, in doing so, they were causing the subjects to experience pain that appeared to be excruciating. While most participants refused to turn the shock-administering knobs to the highest setting, the percentage of participants who continued to comply with the orders, even after it became apparent that they were causing the so-called subjects pain, was far greater than had been expected. The prediction had been that most would refuse to comply almost immediately after it became apparent that they were causing the subjects pain. After all, it was originally thought, how else would morally decent individuals behave?

The experiment, conducted at Yale University, is a superb example of how thinking can be skewed when social reality is seen through the lenses of a very powerful ideal—the Socratic ideal, in this case. The implicit assumption, going into the experiment, was that the average morally decent citizen is but a Socrates in miniature. The experiment did not appreciate the legitimate authority invested in the name of both science and Yale University. It was sheer folly to suppose that the ordinary working-class citizen in America would readily stand up to these institutions, given any ambivalence between the citizen's own assessment of things and the institutional authority's assessment; moreover, the participants' belief that they were cooperating in a legitimate scientific endeavor would incline them to set aside their own evaluation of things. After all, how can the assessment of an ordinary citizen have much weight against the authority of science in the form of Yale University, except perhaps in the case of a direct and explicit conflict with a religious conviction? The behavior being asked of the participants seemed untoward, but how could it really be wrong if it was being required by science and its representative, Yale University? As one writer put it: "In order to persuade a good moral man to do evil, then, it is not necessary first to persuade him to become evil. It is only necessary to teach him that he is doing good."[7]

As with immoral rapprochement, the phenomenon of obedience to authority gives us insight into how morally decent people can be moved to perform immoral behavior: 1. The behavior at issue must be morally embellished so that it does not appear to conflict in a direct and explicit way with a deeply held moral conviction, or with the requirements of another institution that has a considerable hold on the performer. 2. The person issuing the order (or making the request) must have clear and unambiguous authority over the person who is to perform the action. Or, in any case, the performer must have little or no authority in the institution represented by the person issuing the order or request. 3. The institution requesting the behavior must play an affirming role for the performer; hence, successfully per-

---

[7]L. W. Doob, *Panorama of Evil* (Westport, Conn.: Greenwood Press, 1978), p. 99.

forming the action in question enhances the performer's self-esteem.

This third condition, I believe, explains why the institution is favored when a performer is ambivalent about the rightness of what is being required of her. It clearly was at work in the Milgram experiment. The ordinary person often takes pride in being associated with science in general or with Ivy League institutions in even the most minimal of ways. The Milgram experiment proved to be monumental in its moral significance. Even had the results been less impressive, however, it would nonetheless have been the opportunity of a lifetime for most of the participants. As far as being associated with either science or Yale was concerned, the experiment offered most of the participants as much of a chance as they could have hoped for. It is no accident that the one participant who, from the very outset, had no difficulty questioning the appropriateness of what was being asked of participants was a faculty member at the divinity school of an Ivy League institution. Although this faculty member might have had all sorts of interesting reasons for participating in the experiment, there can be little doubt that doing so was not going to enhance this person's self-esteem. For this person, the experiment was surely not the opportunity of a lifetime.

4. *Obeying Authority and Becoming Morally Sullied*

Suppose a person is wearing a spotless pair of white pants. No doubt the person will be very concerned to keep them that way, paying careful attention to where he sits, to how he handles his food, and so on. Now, suppose a child accidentally spills orange soda on the man's pants, leaving a few orange spots at the bottom of both pant legs. Although the spots are barely noticeable and the pants could certainly be much dirtier, the threshold has been broken: the pants are no longer spotless. If another child should accidentally spill some chocolate soda, spattering a few drops on the bottom of both pant legs, the trousers will become even more soiled. Just so, no threshold will have been broken in this latter instance. The first incident ruined any hope that the man had of going through the day without getting any spots on the white pants. The second incident was beside the point, though it might have ruined the hope that the pants would not get any dirtier. One imagines, though, that it is the first hope that really mattered. In fact, one can imagine that the man might very well be indifferent to the second spill, since it was only the first spots that marked a sharp qualitative difference with respect to keeping the pants clean. To be sure, the man might be equally distraught over the second spill; this is not likely, though, if only for the reason mentioned in the preceding sentence. What cannot be said, in any case, is that if the man is not bothered by the second spill, then he was not all that interested in keeping the pants spotless in the first place.

One can imagine that many a participant in the Milgram experiment vowed never to be caught up in that situation again. Milgram tells us that all but a few left genuinely and deeply troubled over having administered ever more potent shocks to the subjects. An offhand response would be that if they had been that troubled, they would not have continued administering more intense shocks. That response fails to take seriously the problem of extricating oneself from a morally objectionable situation when others have been witness to one's morally wrong actions. Psychologically, the extrication is often much easier if one has not become sullied in the first place. The reason is that in the eyes of witnesses the moral persuasiveness of an objection to participating in a situation is radically diminished on account of having become sullied. One's moral leverage, if you will, is radically diminished. It becomes difficult to insist that one is not like other participants or that one has no interest in participating in the wrong behavior. And while there is certainly a moral difference between participating once in a morally wrong activity and then refusing to repeat it, the distinction does not have nearly the rhetorical moral force of the difference between participating once in a morally wrong activity and not doing so at all.

The observations just made hold when a person's participation in a morally wrong activity takes place among equals. Understandably, they hold even more so when the person who has become sullied is in a subordinate role with respect to the witnesses. For the person is then lacking in leverage on two accounts, socially and morally. This consideration can be seen as an extension of the remarks made in the concluding paragraph of the preceding section. Given the social standing of the vast majority of the participants in the Milgram experiment, they were at a disadvantage to begin with in terms of saying no once they had arrived upon the scene. And their becoming sullied only aggravated matters. That is why there seems to have been very nearly an anxiety crisis in almost every case when the participant called the experiment to a halt before administering the highest level of shock. Having no leverage with the experimenters, the participants simply continued until they became sufficiently uncomfortable with themselves.

It is significant that there was perhaps no other way for the participants to extricate themselves from the situation, for the task, namely, turning a knob, was far too simple for anyone to feign incompetence. No one could claim to discover that her ability to turn a knob was no longer what it used to be! And while a physical ailment like arthritis can truly get in the way of performing tasks that require dexterity, steadiness of hand, or strength of fingers, no one could really hope to excuse himself from turning a knob by citing arthritis.

When we are among others with whom we lack leverage, one of the most important means of avoiding participation in a morally wrong activity is the appeal to incompetence. While the matter is speculative, there is reason enough to believe, given the level of discomfort that many of the participants felt, that Milgram would have gotten quite different results had it been possible for the participants to feign incompetence at the task required of them. It would seem that many of them were morally decent people who were surprised by their own complicity in what they came to be convinced was wrongdoing. To be sure, given the Socratic ideal, the participants ought to have had the moral wherewithal just to say no, either from the very start or, certainly, the minute they became convinced of the wrongfulness of their behavior. I have drawn attention to factors, taken in conjunction with one another, that explain why this expectation was unreasonable in the case of the Milgram experiment: the first having to do with the way in which we are socialized to respect legitimate authority; the second having to do with the lack of moral leverage, especially on account of one's own behavior having been sullied.

So consider the thesis that the best way to live a moral life is not to do anything morally wrong. The thesis turns out not to be as trivial as one might first suppose. When we become morally sullied in ways that exceed an ordinary moral faux pas, a psychological threshold is crossed. And getting back across that threshold takes more effort than not crossing it in the first place; indeed, the return journey is not always made. There is often delay, in any case. Becoming sullied, then, is a morally significant threshold. While there are obviously many ways in which this can come about, one of them, of course, is through the phenomenon of immoral rapprochement itself.

My aim in this chapter has been to show, in a rather intuitive way, that we need hardly suppose that human beings are innately evil in order to make sense of how evil can gain a foothold in our lives. To deny the very possibility of moral innocence is, in effect, to assume precisely the matter that needs to be explained. The fragility–goodness model, by allowing that much can go wrong, takes seriously both the possibility of moral innocence and the reality of the human condition. More important, the model takes seriously the possibility of innocence without ever flying in the face of the reality of evil. The fragility–goodness model is compatible with all the evil that we see. If all parents should shamefully abuse their children, as a result of which we would have a world of highly dysfunctional children, the result would not alter the fact that children flourish with loving parents. Moreover, we would have a sound explanation for why it is that so many children are indeed dysfunctional. So it is with the fragility–goodness model of the human condition. The model tells us what surely we all know at some level, namely that neither moral goodness nor moral evil occurs in a social vacuum, but that the occurrence of either is very much contingent upon the social intricacies of human life. Any theory of the human condition that invites us to ignore this truth does more harm than good.

The fragility–goodness model enables us to make a great deal of sense of how evil can gain a foothold in the lives of ordinary people who have moral aspirations without, in the first place, casting a pall of suspicion on the goodness of their moral character. Yet, at the same time, the model does not readily absolve anyone from moral blame—an insuperable problem for the innate-evil model. With the fragility–goodness model before us, I turn in the chapter that follows to the specific case of the moral community. Let me repeat that I have not sought to justify evil, but to make sense of how we can get from a measure of innocence to evil.[8]

---

[8] In writing this chapter, I am especially indebted to Martha Nussbaum, *The Fragility of Goodness* (New York: Cambridge University Press, 1986) and Nancy Sherman, *The Fabric of Character* (New York: Oxford University Press, 1989).

The Moral Community

A community is not simply a collection of individuals residing in a limited and well-defined geographical space. Like a large choir, the whole of a community is greater than, or certainly different from, the mere sum of its members. The choir analogy is most apt, for while in most instances each voice by itself is of little importance, there can be no doubt that taking away a number of voices of little importance in themselves will have a disastrous result for the choir. No voice alone, however beautiful, can produce a sound of harmony. No voice, however mellifluous, can produce the richness of quality that a hundred voices can when singing so softly that they are barely audible.

A conviction, however strong, does not make a consensus. That takes at least two people. As John Stuart Mill saw as clearly as anyone, nothing can take the place of widespread community consensus; and nothing has a greater bearing upon our public conduct than community consensus, if only because no one can afford to offend everyone. This chapter explores one of the ways in which a particular kind of community moral consensus, referred to as laissez-faire common-sense morality, can be a significant factor in the occurrence of evil. Thus, what follows is not a recommendation but a description, developed with an eye toward understanding how it is possible for evil to occur.

As its name suggests, laissez-faire common-sense morality is a particular conception of common-sense morality. Other kinds of common-sense morality would be Aristotelian or Kantian or Christian. In any event, laissez-faire common-sense morality has its roots in classical liberalism of the sort that Mill defended, and expressions of it can be found in contemporary liberalism.[1] An important difference between the two schools of thought is that Mill appealed to a rich conception of human nature, whereas contemporary liberalism tends not to do so. But liberalism, of either variety, is not my concern as such. I offer instead an account of laissez-faire common-sense morality, which I do not claim to be a perfectly consistent doctrine. However, since I shall not be discussing any conception of common-sense morality save the laissez-faire one, I shall refer to the laissez-faire concept as simply common-sense morality.

5. Common-Sense Morality

Our moral duty is not so much to help strangers as it is not to harm them.[2] This, at any rate, is the message of laissez-faire common-sense morality, or laissez-faire folk morality, as I shall sometimes call it. People are not morally required to inconvenience themselves, or in any way to make themselves worse off, for the purpose of helping strangers. The duty to help, common-

[1] See J. Stuart Mill, *On Liberty*. For a statement of contemporary liberalism that is now a classic, see John Rawls, *A Theory of Justice* (Cambridge: Harvard University Press, 1971).

[2] The best brief statement of what I have called laissez-faire common-sense morality can be found in Judith Jarvis Thomson, "A Defense of Abortion," *Philosophy and Public Affairs* 1 (1971). Some think that she is offering a libertarian defense of abortion. This is not the place to debate the matter.

sense morality tells us, is reserved for friends and, especially, family members. Of course, common-sense morality allows that it would be kind of anyone to offer assistance to a stranger, and a person might in fact obligate herself to assist strangers; this conception of morality hardly denies that benevolence and charity are virtues. Just so, it does not require that one offer assistance to strangers except perhaps when the assistance needed is minimal and risk-free, and when giving aid would have a very negligible effect upon one's resources, while making a most significant difference to the recipient. Anyone who could save a person's life simply by calling the police for assistance should do so. Or, one should surely give an individual a dollar, instead of spending it on a soda, if right then and there one could actually make the difference between that person's living and dying. Common-sense morality is rather vague about the circumstances of when we should help strangers, but it is clear that our obligation to do so is extremely limited. Quite simply: The stranger has very little claim to our assistance. To go substantially out of one's way to help a stranger, to dig deep into one's pocket, or to risk one's very life for this purpose is to go beyond the call of duty—so it is held by common-sense morality.

Thus, common-sense morality draws a sharp distinction between family members and friends, on the one hand, and those not close to us, on the other. In fact, it distinguishes sharply between friends and mere acquaintances. I shall not be discussing the obligations that family members and friends have toward one another. I am interested exclusively in the obligations among those who are strangers, according to common-sense morality. This distinction should be understood throughout when I speak about the obligations of persons to persons or persons to strangers. With the possible exception of acquaintances, I think that, for all practical purposes, any relationship other than that of family members and friendships can be treated on the model of strangers. There is no need to define these categories. It suffices that on almost any reasonable account of friendship, most people will have far fewer friends than there are members of the surrounding population. Hence, it stands to reason that most people will be strangers to one another. This will be so even in the case of someone who is widely admired, since admiration, while obviously compatible with friendship, does not entail friendship.

Folk morality allows that there is a difference between offering material resources and offering nonrisky physical assistance to help others, and is considerably less demanding of us in terms of the former. Anyone who can afford to spend three thousand dollars on a vacation every year can probably afford to help the financially needy. But folk morality does not require this form of assistance, although it does seem to require that we make a phone call if that can save another's life or that we throw a rope into the pool to prevent a drowning.

The difference in demands on us is tied to two considerations. First, there is the idea that only rarely are persons morally required to make themselves worse off in order to help a stranger. Second, a distinction is drawn between repertoire-type goods and depletion-type goods. Nonrisky physical assistance is of the repertoire type: Whenever a person offers nonrisky physical assistance, she is not on that account alone left with fewer instances of nonrisky physical assistance to offer, any more than a person who says hello is left with one less hello to utter. Material resources, on the other hand, are obviously depletion-type goods: Whenever a person gives some material resource to another, that act leaves her with less of the resource than she would otherwise have had. If the person gives up only a meager amount of the resource, then for all practical purposes the loss does not make her worse off. Someone who starts out with ten thousand dollars (or even as little as a hundred dollars) is not for all practical purposes really worse off for giving a dollar (or a penny) to someone else. And folk morality says that anyone with the original sum of money should certainly give a dollar (or a penny) to another if it meant the difference between that person's living or dying. But it is obviously rare for so meager an amount to make such a dramatic difference in a person's life. And when a meager amount will simply not suffice, folk morality does not require the gift of whatever sum that would make a difference in the lives of others. Nor are persons required to give time and time again even a meager amount that would make a dramatic difference in a single case if there are endless demands for the same small sum. Oxfam, for instance, tells us that a mere ten dollars will save a life. The dilemma in responding is that there are literally millions of lives that need to be saved.

There is a third condition in giving assistance, namely proximity. Folk morality does not require individuals to seek out the opportunity to do what is beneficial to others, including saving a life. What folk morality insists is that an individual act to save a person's life if the opportunity to do so should present itself directly and if the costs or risks are minimal. If, during a relaxing afternoon on the beach, a physician who is an excellent swimmer should see a child drowning, surely the swimmer should make an attempt to save the child's life, assuming that the water is safe and other conditions permit. But the physician need not travel great distances for the purpose of saving a human life. Nor does folk morality require her to wire money to the family on the other side of the state who (as she has seen on her portable television) have lost their home to an arsonist, even though she has plenty of money. On the other hand, she might be expected to offer some assistance, monetary or otherwise, should her next-door neighbor suffer a like fate. It would be quite callous of her not to offer some assistance to her neighbor, but not so in the case of the person on the other side of the state. (How folk morality understands the concept of callousness is explored in the next section.)

Not surprisingly, folk morality distinguishes quite sharply between failing to help a person and doing harm to a person: The failure to help another is not tantamount to harming that person although doing harm to a person is, of course, not of help to her or him. One does not harm a person even if one could easily offer assistance but fails to do so. Accordingly, folk morality rejects the view that the moral status of an act and of an omission are identical if the consequences of each are the same and if the intentions behind each are the same. For common-sense morality maintains that, however horrible it might be to let something bad happen to another because one delights in the person's suffering, this nonetheless falls short—if only by a hair's breadth, in some cases—of actually causing something bad to happen to that person. To let one's baby drown in the bath—that is, to stand by and watch it do so—in the hope of obtaining thereby a large inheritance is undeniably monstrous.[3] But physical action intended to drown the infant is worse still, or so folk morality tells us. In the latter instance, one is the causal agent in its death. One does not merely fidget while the infant thrashes about in the water; in the hope that it will die, one acts to bring about its death by drowning. I shall sketch in a moment the view that folk morality holds regarding the connection between intentions and omissions.

Naturally, high ideals are very much a part of common-sense morality. People do what is most commendable in selling all that they have in order to help the poor. But sainthood is one thing; ordinary moral decency is another. The latter is required of persons, while the former is not. And the ordinary morally decent person is, foremost, one who does not harm others—specifically, one who is not the causal agent in others' being worse off. Next, the ordinary morally decent person is willing to offer aid if nonrisky assistance is required or if a meager amount of a resource will make a dramatic positive difference but will not put the person under further obligation.

[3]This example is taken from James Rachels's paper "Active and Passive Euthanasia," *New England Journal of Medicine* 292 (1975).

Now I have perhaps given the impression that folk morality has nothing to say about desires but addresses only behavior—that, in particular, an ordinary morally decent person can have any desires whatsoever as long as the person is not the causal agent in anyone's being worse off. Not so, however. Folk morality is clear that the ordinary morally decent person has no desire to harm others and takes no delight in the suffering of others. Nonetheless, under this conception of the ordinary morally decent person (or ordinary moral person, as I shall sometimes say), one who desires to harm others but refrains from doing so is a morally better person than one who acts on such a desire. The one who refrains is an ordinary, morally decent individual, if only barely so. If nothing else, such a person exercises sufficient self-restraint so as not to act on the desire to harm others. And this, common-sense morality maintains, is certainly to the individual's credit.

Common-sense morality's view of the ordinary morally decent individual has its roots in a number of considerations.[4] One of these is that whether or not we can control the desires we come to have, we certainly can control whether or not we act on them. Owing to a variety of factors, we sometimes have morally objectionable desires in spite of our best efforts not to do so. Another consideration is that the task of doing no harm to others is quite manageable and nonburdensome, in that it can be universally satisfied all at once, whereas the task of helping others is quite onerous, requiring that one extend oneself time and time again. A third has to do with the notion of autonomy. The idea here is that the autonomy of persons is preserved only if the nonchosen, obligatory claims to which they must answer are kept to a minimum. In other words, it is impossible to live an autonomous life if one must give oneself over to meeting the needs of others

---

[4]Here I draw upon Richard Trammell's forceful essay "Saving Life and Taking Life," *Journal of Philosophy* 72 (1975).

unless, of course, it is precisely that sort of life that one has chosen.[5] The fourth consideration to be mentioned concerns the nature of human beings. It seems clear that human beings are by no means wholly altruistic, any more than they are wholly self-interested. Thus, the duty to help strangers would seem to require that people identify with the good of others far more than they have the psychological wherewithal to do so.

Yet another consideration that supports common-sense morality's conception of the ordinary moral person has to do with supererogation, the idea of going beyond the call of duty in acting for the good of another. Common-sense morality thus takes it to be good that individuals go beyond what is morally required of them in dealing with others. A more morally demanding conception of the person would erode the space between what is supererogatory and what is morally required. With common-sense morality, however, most positive acts of virtue of great significance are supererogatory.

I do not claim that, when subject to critical scrutiny, folk morality's conception of the ordinary moral person can be seen to flow from the foregoing considerations. Nor shall I be concerned here to show whether or not this is so. My claim is only that these are the sorts of considerations that, offhand, are often thought to lend plausibility to folk morality's conception of the ordinary moral person. In the final analysis, they may not do so at all.

I remarked at the outset that I do not hold that common-sense morality is a formally consistent doctrine. There are philosophers who are persuaded that there is no morally significant difference to be found between acts and omissions when both the consequences and the intentions are the same. Whether or not these philosophers are correct, however, ordinary people do see a

<hr />

[5]For an eloquent statement of this view, see Jean Blumenfeld, "Causing Harm and Bringing Aid," *American Philosophical Quarterly* 18 (1981).

morally significant difference between such acts and omissions. And I am interested in capturing what the ordinary person thinks about such matters, not what the best philosophical theory might be.

As I have already noted, folk morality denies that an act and an omission should receive the same moral evaluation although the intentions and the consequences are the same. Even when one is aware of an individual's suffering and can offer assistance, folk morality denies that omitting to help entails a desire to see that person suffer. Logically this is quite correct, for it is possible to be simply indifferent to a person's plight, desiring neither to help the person nor to see the person become worse off. In this regard, a distinction should be drawn between what we might call callous indifference and distracted indifference. The former is the reaction of a callous person; the latter is the response of a noncallous person who is distracted in some way that prevents her or him from being moved by the suffering of the person at hand. The callous person seems to be very nearly as bad as the person who delights in another's suffering and who is thus condemned by folk morality. Presumably anyone who watches an innocent baby drown in a tub of water, citing as grounds that whether the baby lives or dies makes no difference to his life one way or the other, is a callous person indeed. And there are times—as in this example of the baby—when it is hard to imagine any reason other than sheer callousness for one person to let another suffer.

But not every case of letting someone suffer instead of offering assistance can be attributed to callous indifference. It is possible for an individual's moral sensibilities to become temporarily deadened to the concerns of another. Let us refer to this condition as distracted indifference.

The person who has just experienced the death of a parent or a child is not likely at the moment to be much moved by the suffering of another. The same holds for the breadwinner of the family who has just lost her job. A major disappointment, an especially harsh comment from a fellow employee or negative appraisal from one's superior, a very unpleasant self-discovery or realization about a friend, and so on can each render one momentarily less receptive—indeed, indifferent—to the concerns of others without signifying in any way that one is a callous individual. Occasions of great joy can have a desensitizing effect as well. On the eve of receiving the offer of her dreams, a professorship at Oxford University, a person, wanting to celebrate, will probably be less concerned with the suffering of others. Likewise for a couple on the occasion of their wedding day. Folk morality acknowledges that there are times when it is quite natural for a person not to be moved by the suffering of another, though she or he could easily offer assistance. At such times, indifference in no way entails that the individual either is callous or desires to see the other suffer. Of course, while some instances of suitable distracted indifference are obvious, others are not. And reasonable people may disagree, in any case, on what is suitable.

What is more, some forms of distracted indifference bespeak a character shortcoming. Suppose a man, terribly vain, is so busy attending to his appearance reflected in the window that the screaming going on in the background does not register as indication of a possible rape. If the screaming had registered, he would have reacted. He is thus hardly indifferent to the moral horror of a rape; he is even willing to run some risks to himself in order to prevent it. It is just that concern with his appearance often results in his being inattentive to what is happening in his environment. If the Queen of England had been passing by during one of his fits with his reflection, he probably would not have noticed her either. We might usefully distinguish between excusable and inexcusable distracted indifference. I have just described an inexcusable distracted indifference.

It is not claimed, however, that this distinction regarding indifference is always sharp and easily drawn, only that there is such a distinction, or so laissez-faire common-sense morality allows.

The distinction between callous and excusable distracted indifference assumes a certain moral psychology, which has its roots in the writings of many British moralists. It holds that the mere eyewitnessing of an innocent person's suffering or direct exposure to it suffices to evoke sympathy and concern for that individual, no matter whom the person might be, unless one's own psychological state is that of deep sorrow or extreme joy owing to a momentous occasion. Of course, if the person suffering is a dear friend or a loved one, the mere knowledge of the pain should arouse considerable sympathy. It should even result in some action on behalf of the individual. The callous person is one in whom the arousal of sympathy systematically does not occur under such circumstances. The excusably distracted person is one in whom this arousal is understandably and naturally blocked from occurring owing to the psychological state of great sorrow or joy occasioned by a recent experience. Returning to the earlier example, the physician who sees on television another's misfortune owing to arson is not in any way directly exposed to the suffering, though the presentation may be vivid enough. She is, on the other hand, directly exposed to her neighbor's pain caused by a fire. If she should return home from the beach to discover that her parents have both been murdered, the physician would surely be excused if she gave no thought to misfortune that her neighbor has just suffered.

I have gone on at length about the laissez-faire conception of common-sense morality in order to make a very important point, namely that, according to this conception, being an ordinary morally decent person is compatible with allowing much harm to go on in the world—harm that, in fact, one could easily help to eliminate. More to the point, this conception of the ordinary morally decent person is compatible with allowing much harm even when people are the causal agents of that harm. For the conception does not require that persons do a great deal to prevent the harm that one person causes another. The reason is that effective assistance is rarely either nonrisky or attainable with meager resources; and common-sense morality does not require that people make themselves worse off in order to prevent harm to others—even harm resulting from agency.

This last point should be restated in a way that brings out its full force: Common-sense morality does not require that people take a stand to prevent the occurrence of evil. It was an admirable thing that, during the civil rights movement, many white youth participated in the sit-in demonstrations at food counters throughout the South. Many of those sit-in demonstrations would have been far less effective had it not been for the whites who gave of themselves for the cause of racial equality. But this commitment was purely altruistic on the part of the whites. Common-sense morality did not require it of them. Again, the civil rights movement might well have taken a different turn had not many Jews put aside promising law careers to work for the NAACP. But, once more, this self-denial was purely altruistic on their part. Common-sense morality did not require it of them. Had they accepted offers from prominent law firms and gone about living their lives and raising families, as anyone might want to do, who could have blamed them? No one, at least not from the standpoint of common-sense morality.

It was no doubt anti-Semitism pure and simple that prevented the United States,[6] as well as other nations, from lifting immigration quotas when, at the Evian Conference, Hitler asked which among the nations convened there would be willing to admit Germany's Jews. On the one hand, no nation was required by common-sense morality to do so. On the other, what

---

[6]See David S. Wyman, *The Abandonment of the Jews: America and the Holocaust, 1941–45* (New York: Pantheon Books, 1984).

might have come to pass had many or most of the nations at the Evian Conference opened their doors to Jews? It is not idle speculation to suppose that Hitler, in that case, might not have proceeded with the Final Solution. For based upon the refusal of any nation to open its doors to the Jews, the message that Hitler took away from that conference is that no one cared about what happened to Jewish people.

At no point have I denied that common-sense morality can applaud those who put themselves out on behalf of others. Rather, my point has been that rarely does folk morality require individuals to make substantial sacrifices for the sake of others, even when much of moral significance hangs in the balance. It is a tribute to their moral character that nonblacks paid dearly during the civil rights movement to advance the cause of social equality in America. It remains the unvarnished truth, however, that common-sense morality had no claim to their doing so, no matter how much it may applaud them.

6. Moral Drift

I turn now to the notion of moral drift. My concern is to bring out that the doctrine of common-sense morality constitutes especially fertile ground for the phenomenon of moral drift. As we shall see, this is no small shortcoming of the doctrine.

We have moral drift when a morally inappropriate piece of behavior that has rarely occurred in society begins to occur with such frequency that a great many members of society now expect it to occur or, at any rate, are no longer surprised when it takes place. Furthermore, society is worse off on account of the greater frequency of the behavior.[7] Obviously, there will be disagree-

---

[7] I borrow here from John Sabini and Maury Silver, *The Moralities of Everyday Life* (New York: Oxford University Press, 1982). The idea of moral drift is theirs. As I have embellished their account and do not know whether they would approve of the embellishments, a caveat is in order. As Sabini and Silver charac-

ment in some instances over whether moral drift has occurred. There are those who would insist that the raising of hemlines in women's dresses or the shift toward androgynous attire or the greater tolerance of homosexuality is each an instance of moral drift. Others would not agree. By contrast, there is no disputing that we have had moral drift as manifested by the increase in crimes of violence. Further, the mayhem on television and the raw viciousness of horror films have been instruments of moral drift if they have desensitized people to real-life violence or have encouraged more violent behavior by fueling the imagination.

Clearly, the notion of moral drift is to be understood by reference to a set of operative moral practices—any such set. Thus, on the continuum of good and evil, there can be moral drift at any point along the way. And what is meant by operative moral practices is the legitimate expectations that people have about how others in society, meaning strangers, will treat them. If, with good reason, people used to feel safe walking alone at night and, with equally good reason, they now feel uneasy, then there has been moral drift with respect to safety at night. Or, if pornography now depicts children with a frequency that was once at least confined to adults, then there has been moral drift with respect to pornography. Few can be unaware that words of bigotry and contempt, once found mainly upon the walls of public restrooms, now deface almost any area of public access; there has been moral drift, then, with respect to the writing of offensive language in public places. Things have gone from the morally bad to the morally worse.

As with any notion, whether we have moral drift or not may be a matter of debate. Still, moral drift is defined so as to rule out certain counterintuitive cases. Suppose a society of people of good will should find themselves doing just a little less good

---

terize the notion, moral drift can be either good or bad. As they use it, however, the term refers to changes that are bad. I follow their usage.

than they used to do. Well, such a slacking off is hardly tantamount to engaging in moral wrongdoing. A society of people of good will might become less commendable without opening themselves to moral criticism. Hence, we do not have moral drift in this instance. Strictly speaking, society is in some sense worse off because less good is being done than before; however, it is not worse off owing to an increase in wrongdoing.

A shift to a less morally commendable state of affairs, though not constituting an instance of moral drift in a strict sense, could nonetheless occasion such drift.

Suppose that people used to make a point of stopping by to visit the homes of the elderly in their neighborhood. Nothing formal about it. Sometimes people stopped by en route to or from some other destination; sometimes an elderly person's home was the destination. A visit could be short or long. But with the advent of the telephone, things began to change. The tradition of looking in on the elderly did not cease immediately, but over the years, fewer and fewer people did so. People would telephone, instead. So far we have an undesirable change, because the elderly really appreciated the spontaneous visits. Even so, we do not have a moral wrong. But suppose that as a result of the less frequent visits, crimes against the elderly rise. Further, people become less and less concerned about what happens to the elderly in the neighborhood, save for family members. We now have moral drift, owing to a shift, unrelated to morality, in the character of social interaction.

Here is another example. VCRs are morally neutral instruments. Yet their advent into society may have contributed to considerable moral drift—if, that is, pornography in any context is morally objectionable. VCRs have made it possible for people to view pornography in privacy, the result being that people who would not consider entering a pornographic theater are nevertheless able to purchase or rent such films for home viewing.

With one more observation we can tie together the claims of this and the preceding section. As John Stuart Mill saw quite well (*Utilitarianism*, ch. 3), moral disapprobation serves as an important check on morally objectionable behavior. Because very few are indifferent to social disapproval, the anticipation of such disapproval is a reason, often a very strong and sometimes sufficient reason, for staying one's hand or biting one's tongue. A person is far less likely to refer to forty-five-year-old women as "girls" or to homosexual men as "faggots" if the terms would meet with widespread disapproval from peers or associates. This is so even if in her heart of hearts the person thinks that there is nothing wrong with such usage. Moral disapproval does not influence everyone. (Virtually nothing does that.) It does, however, make a difference to the vast majority of people. A great many people would often rather watch their words than lose face. Naturally, it would be much better if a person refrains from doing what is wrong—especially a grave wrong—because he believes it to be immoral. But failing that, better that a person refrains for fear of public outrage than that he not refrain at all.

Mill's point, of course, was not that people are chafing at the bit to act immorally, or that they act morally only because they desire to avoid social disapproval, though these observations are undoubtedly true in some instances. Nor did he seem to think it desirable that people act morally only out of fear of disapproval. Rather, it seems that Mill can be understood as making two weaker, but very significant, points. First, when the will to do right is weakened, as might naturally be the case for anyone from time to time, the desire to avoid social disapproval can very often be the stop that plugs the dam, thereby making it possible for persons to resist until the temptation passes, and thus stay the moral course. Second, the will of persons to do what is right is generally affected by the character of the moral climate in which they live; it is the very rare person, indeed, who can maintain the highest moral standards in the context of an evil social environment. It is increasingly difficult to sustain the will to do what is right and good in an environment where doing the right and the good is roundly unappreciated.

We can powerfully illustrate this with the sentiment of gratitude. It is doubtful that gratitude alone tips the scales in favor of acting on behalf of others. And surely no morally decent person should assist others only for sake of their gratitude. All the same, blatant ingratitude can be a decisive factor against acting on behalf of a person. Gratitude is an individual's acknowledgment of the good that another has done for him, especially the good intentions and willingness with which the deed was done. Thus, ingratitude is a form of ill will that constitutes something of an affront to the agent's character, in that the good intentions and willingness with which he acted on the other's behalf are denied or in some way discredited by the other person. Understandably, an individual who is in no way motivated by the desire to be the object of another's gratitude will nonetheless not want to have his good intentions discredited, just as a person whose truth telling is not motivated by the desire to be praised as an honest person will nonetheless not want her words wrongly discredited as lies. Accordingly, a person may find it preferable not to act on another's behalf at all if the person's good intentions are to be the object of the other's ill will. It is offensive when manifestly good intentions are greeted with ill will.

Thus, should there be any righteous people in an evil moral climate, it is very unlikely that they would continue doing good for long if their deeds were generally greeted with ingratitude or scorn. In refraining from doing good for others, not even the righteous are immune to the effects of an evil moral climate. They may not in fact do evil themselves, but the odds are that they will do less good.

These observations sharpen our understanding of the character of moral drift. The phenomenon should not be understood as stemming from a well-entrenched desire on the part of the vast majority of people to do what is wrong. On this construal, an erosion of public disapproval of wrongdoing would seem to be almost inevitable. Rather, the phenomenon of moral drift can be caused by a multitude of factors, including amoral forces that have a deleterious effect upon the character of social interaction.

There is, then, an extremely important asymmetry between evil and good.[8] No matter how commendable a moral climate might be, if an evil person is introduced into that environment, the moral climate may not prevent that individual from doing what is morally wrong, from the trivial to the heinous. A morally good climate does not in any way make a lie, theft, or murder less worthwhile for the wrongdoer. The wrong of a lie or a theft is not diminished in the absence of suspicion that the agent has so behaved. In fact, from the agent's point of view that may be the preferable state of affairs. More poignantly, a commendable moral environment does not make most evil acts less attractive for lack of appreciation of their evilness, as it were, by righteous people. For an agent of evil, there is nothing parallel to ingratitude that serves to make doing evil unattractive in the way that ingratitude can make doing good unattractive to an agent of good.

The closest we get to a parallel here is revenge. To be sure, one can take revenge upon a person without her knowing who caused her harm, but there can be no doubt that revenge is sweeter to the agent when the target knows that he indeed com-

---

[8]For a lovely statement of the asymmetry between good and evil, see Gregory Curtis, "Why Evil Attracts Us," in Paul Woodruff and Harry A. Wilmer, *Facing Evil: Light at the Core of Darkness* (LaSalle, Ill.: Open Court, 1988). He writes: "There are other reasons why evil is attractive. We must search for the good while evil seeks us out. In Eden, Eve did not go looking for the serpent; rather, it came to her. Evil accepts us. It does not require us to improve. No matter how great our faults, evil will embrace us. Evil validates our weaknesses and our secret appetites. It tells us that we're all right" (p. 94).

mitted the harm against her. Revenge is fueled not only by the desire to get even, but also by the desire that the victim realize that one has gotten even with her. Hence, it is characteristic of a person seeking revenge to leave a telltale sign, even if the sign should do no more than invite the suspicion that he was the agent of revenge. In fact, while one may not want to do any more than invite suspicion, one may be adamant about doing exactly that.

Against this alleged asymmetry it might be objected that the morally decent person does good for its own sake. Of course, the person appreciates gratitude; but if, so the objection goes, the absence of gratitude would serve to stay his hand, then what this shows is not that there is an asymmetry between morality and evil, but that the person in question is not as morally decent as he makes himself out to be. While this objection is not without a point, I fear that it misses the mark. To be sure, there is much moral good that morally decent individuals do in which seeking to be an object of gratitude is entirely beside the point. Acts of generalized charity come readily to mind, such as gifts to the Red Cross (in the form of either money or blood donations), United Way, and the like. Such acts of charity are often anonymous, and even when they are not, the benefits are usually distributed by and in the name of an organization rather than in the names of individual donors. Without question, a morally decent person would engage in generalized acts of charity, and concerns of gratitude would have no bearing on the matter. As it happens, though, generalized acts of charity do not even begin to exhaust the landscape of the morally good. There is a wealth of morally good deeds that are essentially interpersonal in character. And in the case of interpersonal goods, ingratitude can be decisive in a decision to refrain from offering assistance.

A good deed is essentially interpersonal in character when all parties to the interaction are aware of who is in need of assistance and who is offering assistance, and when there is at least the presumption that the assistance being offered is welcomed. Although the proverbial helping an elderly person across the street comes readily to mind here, interpersonal good deeds take place between all sorts of individuals, and range from trivial favors to major acts of good will to acts of self-sacrifice. Keeping a watch on the neighbors' house, at their request, is an interpersonal good deed, as is making a personal loan to a friend. Telling a stranger who is walking away from his parked car that he left his car lights on is an interpersonal good deed. Preventing a rape or running into a burning building to save a life or letting others escape first in a situation that is equally life threatening to everyone are all paradigm examples of interpersonal good deeds.

With the accounts of both common-sense morality and moral drift before us, we are now in a position to draw some connections—to see, in particular, the implications that the former has for the latter. While moral drift is no doubt possible in almost any moral context, some such contexts are more fertile ground for its occurrence than others. It stands to reason, surely, that moral drift is more likely to occur in a context where the conception of the good person is based on common-sense morality than in a context where the conception is determined by the ideals of sainthood—for instance, where taking an interest in the well-being of others is held to be at the very core of moral decency. For, other things equal, given any two moral contexts, the occurrence of moral drift is favored in the one where the shift from morally bad to morally worse does not readily reflect negatively upon the conception that persons have of themselves as ordinary moral individuals. And this will undoubtedly be true if refraining from harming others is the defining characteristic of being an ordinary moral individual.

We have moral drift if those who rob no longer leave the victims whole, as they once did, but murder them as well. Though ordinary moral individuals, as defined by folk morality, will certainly deplore this shift, they will not see it as calling into question the extent to which they themselves measure up as morally decent individuals. Indeed, it will be no less true that they have refrained from harming anyone, notwithstanding this change for the worse. Although many poverty-stricken neighborhoods are being made even worse by the onslaught of drugs, it hardly occurs to most people that they are being any less the morally decent individuals that they take themselves to be. After all, they do not use drugs.

If not harming others is at the very core of ordinary moral decency, as in common-sense morality, then it is possible to maintain that standard of moral decency, without loss of moral face, in the midst of situations that are morally worsening for others. The situation of others may worsen without our having in any way a contributory role in its doing so, at least not as we understand the notion of a contributory role.

It is precisely because common-sense morality is compatible with our view of ourselves as morally decent in the face of morally worsening situations for others that this moral conception is such fertile soil for moral drift. Neither monitoring what others do nor responding constructively to adverse effects upon others is a defining feature of the demands of common-sense morality.

My claim is that with common-sense morality we have especially fertile soil for the phenomenon of moral drift. I have not claimed that whenever a society embraces common-sense morality, that set of beliefs will be the sole explanation for why things change for the worse morally in the event that they do. Things may change for the worse because individuals are overwhelmed by the cares of life. A family in the clutch of extreme financial difficulties may understandably lack the emotional resources to fight the ever-worsening crime situation in its neighborhood. Another family may be doing all that it can do to cope with a most debilitating illness among its members. Indeed, another family may be emotionally devastated by being a victim of the latest crime wave. There can be a multitude of excusable reasons, having nothing to do with moral drift itself, why individuals do not rise up and confront the wrongdoing that occurs around them; and the failure of individuals, for venial reasons, to stand up to wrongdoing will surely be part of the explanation for why things change for the worse. None of this, however, militates against the connection I have drawn between common-sense morality and moral drift: The former is very fertile soil for the latter.

It will be remembered that the conception of common-sense morality that we have been discussing is laissez-faire in nature. That any conception of common-sense morality should be very fertile soil for moral drift is clearly a very significant feature about that conception. I should imagine that it will come as quite a surprise to many that this claim can be made about the laissez-faire conception of common-sense morality

7. The People of Le Chambon

The people of Le Chambon provide us with a beautiful illustration of many of the claims of this chapter. Their story stands as one of the most beautiful and compelling accounts of good will in the history of humankind.[9]

[9]I follow the account of the Chambonnais to be found in Philip Hallie's *Lest Innocent Blood Be Shed: The Story of the Village of Le Chambon and How Goodness Happened There* (New York: Harper and Row, 1979). I am not concerned to add anything to the historical account of the people of Le Chambon. I want rather to capture some of the spirit of their deeds from a strictly moral perspective. While the people of Le Chambon may be the most famous for the many Jews whom they saved, others also risked their lives to save Jews, of course. See, for example, André Stein's *Quiet Heroes: True Stories of the Rescue of Jews by Christians in Nazi-Occupied Holland* (New York: New York University Press, 1988). For an important philosophical discussion of such matters, see Lawrence Blum, "Moral Exemplars: Reflections on Schindler, the Trocmes, and Others," *Midwest Studies in Philosophy* 13 (1988).

As is well known, the people of this village in France saved the lives of thousands of Jews in defiance of Nazi Germany, at considerable risk to themselves. While we are quick to think of them as heroes, and rightly so, it is striking that they were not much inclined to think of themselves in this way. And while we naturally think of those who risk their lives for others, especially strangers, as going considerably beyond the call of duty and thus doing what is supererogatory, once again it is striking that the people of Le Chambon were not much inclined to think of themselves in this way. What is more, this does not in the least appear to be false modesty on their part.

On the contrary, the villagers quite sincerely believed that in saving the lives of Jews they were doing precisely what a decent person—who is a decent Christian—should be doing. Astoundingly, perhaps, it appears that they could no more have thought not to help a Jew who knocked on their door than they could have thought neither to attend church services on Sunday, nor to lend a neighbor a cup of sugar, nor to tend to their farms. Their view of themselves in relation to others was quite simple: One does not turn a person in need away from one's door, regardless of who that individual might be. They were Christians who took the Christian message of doing good for others at face value. Helping others in need was thus an integral part of their lives. Neither special occasions nor ceremony was required.

The attitude that the people of Le Chambon had toward helping others was rather like the attitude that those whose lives embody the views of folk morality have toward not harming others. Not killing or stealing is, according to folk morality, precisely what a decent person does. To measure up to this level is not something to boast about. Nor is measuring up in this regard anything for which the ordinary person, under ordinary circumstances, deserves special mention or praise. And it would be quite odd for anyone to expect such recognition. To be sure, the circumstances are not always ordinary; and folk morality certainly allows for this. Imagine a drug addict who resolves to go clean after stealing regularly to support her habit. She shows real determination when, in the grip of the tormenting desire for the drug, she refrains from what would have been quite an easy theft for her. Her not stealing in this instance is a testimony to her resolve to go clean, for which she deserves praise. On the other hand, when she has been free of drugs for ten years, her not stealing for drugs, or anything else, will be what one rightly expects of her. For the people of Le Chambon, helping someone in need was rightly expected.

Clearly it would be an egregious understatement to characterize what the people of Le Chambon did as merely offering assistance to the Jews; for they unquestionably saved the lives of thousands upon thousands of Jews. What is more, they did so at great risk to themselves. And the people of Le Chambon were in no way unclear about the nature of their actions, as when a person thinks that he is only turning on a light but, unbeknown to him, is also scaring away a would-be burglar. Yet, not only did the people of Le Chambon not see themselves as doing anything spectacular, but they insisted that their role in saving the lives of so many Jews was something that more or less just happened. This is not easy to understand. Even allowing for a measure of understatement, as perhaps modesty requires, a town does not just happen to save the lives of tens of thousands of people.[10]

While it would surely be foolish to suppose that one could

---

[10]André Stein writes of the rescuers whom he met at a conference on "Righteous Gentiles," in honor of those who rescued Jews: "I was touched by the self-effacing shyness, the awkward bewilderment on these time- and weather-beaten faces. While these people expressed gratitude for the recognition they received, they seemed lost and ill at ease. In their judgment, the celebration of their particular version of heroism was largely misplaced and overstated. 'Since when does a man deserve praise from the highest human sources for being just that, a man?' Some voiced this question in muffled voices, others wore it silently on their puzzled faces" (pp. 5–6).

entirely explain what happened in Le Chambon, let me make the following observation. It is very difficult to take a person into one's home for the purpose of offering him food and warmth, and then turn him out in the full knowledge that his enemies are out there seeking to kill him; for knowingly turning a person out to face killers after feeding him would make a mockery out of doing the former. Better not to do the former at all than to do it and then turn around and do the latter. And it is the former, to begin with, that the people of Le Chambon simply could not leave undone, any more than they could have avoided helping a member of their town in need.

Consider, now, that the morally decent person, even under common-sense morality, does not start each day deliberating about and then reaffirming her commitment not to murder or steal; for not doing these things is second nature to her. Not murdering or stealing is simply a part of her life—not something about which she must deliberate in any regular way. From the standpoint of daily living, not doing these wrongs just happens. Likewise, for the people of Le Chambon, helping others in need was simply a part of their life. I suggest that they gave no more thought to feeding the Jews and providing them with shelter than the morally decent person, from the standpoint of common-sense morality, gives any thought to not murdering or stealing. And in so doing, the villagers found themselves in the context of a deeper moral commitment. But since this deeper moral commitment simply followed in the wake of the other moral commitments, there is a sense in which it also required no thought from the people of Le Chambon. It is not that they were unaware of the consequences of their actions. Rather, because it was unthinkable for them not to feed the hungry, and then unthinkable for them to give food but not refuge, it was also unthinkable not to give refuge. It was not necessary to deliberate about either.

Now, it is common enough for people to find it unthinkable

not to do a certain thing, if they have first done something else—that is, for people not to deliberate about doing one thing, given that they have done another. Having given birth, a woman often finds it unthinkable not to go on to raise the child. She does not much deliberate about this. Having stopped a rape, a rescuer generally finds it unthinkable not to go on to offer comfort to the victim. Staying to give comfort is something that follows naturally. It would be the rare person indeed who, having interrupted a rape, must also debate whether she should stay and comfort the victim rather than keep an appointment, say. Staying to comfort the victim is what one does, virtually whatever one's plans might have been; and most people would find it odd that anyone should think otherwise or that it would even be a matter of deliberation. Yet, interrupting a rape and staying to comfort the victim are clearly two very different acts.

From the standpoint of common-sense morality, what was unusual about the people of Le Chambon, then, is not that they found it unthinkable not to do some things in the wake of having done other things, since that it is common enough. Rather, it is the content of their initial commitments that was so unusual, especially given the circumstances. For it will be remembered that from the standpoint of common-sense morality, opening one's doors to feed others is quite commendable, but one is hardly expected to have a commitment to doing so. And if opening one's doors to feed others meant putting one's own life or the lives of loved ones at risk, then, a fortiori, a person would not be expected to do so. It is certainly one thing for it to be unthinkable not to take a person in to feed him when doing so involves no risk whatsoever to either one's own life or the lives of loved ones; it is another thing entirely when doing so has dire consequences. For the people of Le Chambon, not feeding the Jews and not offering them shelter were unthinkable in spite of the dire consequences of doing so. They knew full well that this put them directly at odds with the objectives of the Third Reich, and that Hitler could be absolutely brutal in his treatment of those who disobeyed his command not to harbor or assist Jews. Yet it remained unthinkable for the villagers not to feed the Jews and offer them shelter. From the standpoint of common-sense morality, this is what is astounding about the people of Le Chambon, as common-sense morality invariably allows that an unassailable excuse for not offering assistance to others, especially complete strangers, is that doing so means jeopardizing the lives of either ourselves or our loved ones. Laissez-faire common-sense morality tells us there is no better excuse for not offering assistance to others, let alone to complete strangers.

Given that it was unthinkable for the people of Le Chambon not to feed and provide the Jews with shelter, in the face of Hitler's explicit orders to the contrary, their willingness to be a haven for the Jews against the Nazis does not seem all that astounding. What would be astounding would be the villagers' refusal to provide a haven after they had risked their lives, in defiance of Hitler, to feed and shelter Jews. This would make no sense.

Obviously, the preceding discussion does not in any way take away from the good that the people of Le Chambon did. However, it does help us to have a sense of how they could have viewed their saving the Jews as something that just happened. There is a sense in which they are quite right about that, given that it was unthinkable for them not to feed the Jews and provide them with shelter in the first place. And that it was unthinkable for them not to do these things in the face of Nazi orders is powerful testimony to what can happen when taking an interest in the well-being of others is a way of life.

Had taking an interest in the well-being of others not been a part of the life of people of Le Chambon long before Hitler came to power, it is very unlikely that they would have had the moral wherewithal to feed and shelter the Jews, not to speak of turning their own homes into a haven, at risk to their own lives. Though much more can be said about the people of Le Chambon, I should like to conclude this chapter with the following general comments. First, the moral expectations that people have of both themselves and others, under ordinary circumstances, are generally tied to the consensus of the moral community in which they live and with which they identify. The moral expectations that exist under ordinary circumstances constitute the baseline, if you will. Second, the way in which a community responds to a grave moral crisis is in general tied to its moral baseline. The lower the baseline, the less likely it is that the community will respond to a grave moral crisis in a morally commendable way; the higher the baseline, the more likely it is that the community will so respond. The community of Le Chambon is an extremely moving example of the extraordinary good that can occur, in response to evil in one of its most threatening forms, when the moral baseline of a community is very high. Suffice it to say that common-sense morality—that is, laissez-faire common-sense morality—has a considerably lower moral baseline. Third, when the moral baseline of a community is exceptionally high, as was the case with the Chambonnais, there is very little room to be ambivalent about helping others in need, because failing to help would be so dramatically at odds with the self-concepts of the members of the community. More often than not, ambivalence is the only window of opportunity that evil needs. If I have argued soundly in characterizing laissez-faire common-sense morality, it perhaps provides evil with more windows of opportunity than many no doubt have been inclined to suppose.

It is, of course, logically possible that a person should, sans self-aggrandizement, put his life on the line for others in the face of a crisis even though no one else in his community would ever think to do so such a thing. Likewise, it is logically possible for a person to be indifferent to the slaughter of innocent persons even though she belongs to a community in which individuals are more than willing to share with others, no matter how little they have. But in fashioning our moral ideals, we must not let the rare and the improbable blind us to the character of moral living for ordinary people and the circumstances that underwrite it.

As the people of Le Chambon make abundantly clear, the way in which a society responds to injustices visited upon others is very much tied to the conception of morality that the society embraces. To be sure, perhaps no society can be expected to embrace a saintly conception of morality, and so open itself to moral criticism for failing to do so. All the same, it should now be clear that, as I have characterized it, common-sense morality yields too low a baseline of moral expectations in a society. Indeed, common-sense morality is widely compatible with compartmentalizations that result in people ignoring the injustices that others are suffering. By way of conclusion, then, common-sense morality has a lower moral baseline than the conception of moral goodness embodied by the fragility–goodness model (introduced in Section 1). In the fragility–goodness model, human beings have a natural capacity for sympathy toward others who are suffering misfortunes and injustices. The prevalence of common-sense morality in societies thus brings out the unsettling truth that societies can embrace a conception of moral goodness that fails to harness fully the natural capacities of persons to be good.

The people of Le Chambon show just how high the moral baseline can go. In the absence of such a high moral baseline, it would have been well-nigh impossible for Jews to have entrusted their very lives into the hands of this Christian community. Alas, it may be that common-sense morality reveals just how low we often allow that baseline to sink without opening ourselves to moral criticism for harming others. It is part of the very fragility of humankind that we often settle for less than the best—not by barely missing the mark but by dramatically lowering our sights and settling for being far less than we could be. The people of Le Chambon serve as a morally beautiful reminder of the richness that life offers when we do not expect so little of ourselves.

Characterizing Evil

It is striking that while theories of the good are legion, philosophers have said precious little about evil outside a theological context.[1] I suggest that an evil act is rather like an Aristotelean virtuous act—that is, an Aristotelean virtuous act turned inside out. I should prefer to talk about evil acts rather than evil events. Events range over moral agents, as well as conditions for which moral agency is impossible or very much a matter of dispute. A world without moral agents would in my view be a world in which evil could not occur, albeit lots of harm would be possible. This move is not meant to be sophistical in any way. From a moral perspective, the only harm worth explaining is the harm that moral agents do, either to other moral agents or to the rest of the world. Unless the harm that falling trees or hurricanes or volcanoes do is attributed to some moral agency in the background, such harm does not admit of a moral explanation, whether the harm be to moral agents, living organisms that are not moral agents, or the rest of the earth.[2] So it is, too, for the

[1]Ronald D. Milo, *Immorality* (Princeton, N.J.: Princeton University Press, 1984); and John Kekes, *Facing Evil* (Princeton, N.J.: Princeton University Press, 1990).

[2]Kekes, *Facing Evil*, initially characterizes evil as undeserved harm. This seems

harm that nonhuman animals do. Moreover, the same holds for harm caused by moral agents when the agent's behavior does not exhibit any agency on the individual's part, negligence aside. Obvious examples of this would be striking someone on account of having an epileptic fit or falling into another on account of having tripped. No moral explanation is called for in either instance. Whether a piece of behavior exhibits agency can, of course, be a matter of dispute. It can even be a matter of dispute whether a living thing is capable of agency. I shall not take up these matters here, though. At the very minimum, then, I take an evil act to be a wrong act that is harmful to another living creature. It goes without saying that I want to allow that some instances of refraining from an act can also be evil, whether they are properly understood as acts or not.

8.   *Acts of Evil*

Obviously, an evil act is not simply a wrong act, since one can do what is wrong quite innocently and unintentionally. Nor is an evil act simply a wrong act that is intentionally committed, although intentions on the part of the agent are necessary for her or his act to be evil. Subway riders who do not pay their fare have an intention to do what is wrong, but it would be a bit much to accuse them of committing an evil deed. The reason is not only that subway systems are more or less faceless things. An individual who steals fifty cents every two months from the till of quite a well-off fellow employee does what is wrong, but not evil. Magnitude is one consideration. Yet evil is not simply a function of the magnitude of harm done. Although a five-year-

---

to get the discussion off on the wrong foot. Indeed, I suggest that this characterization makes it more difficult than he realizes to talk about purely secular evil rather than religious or metaphysical evil.

old who accidentally sets off a series of nuclear weapons that destroy North America causes a harm of unparalleled magnitude, it cannot be plausibly argued that the child did what was evil or that she acted evilly, though the child has certainly caused a great tragedy. Evil is always tragic, but not the converse.

Nor is evil simply a function of the magnitude of harm that results when a person willfully does what is wrong. A mischievous individual may mean to give the old folks in the nursing home a bit of a fright, which is certainly wrong of him to do. But while he intended merely to play a tasteless prank on them, the result of his prank is that in a chain reaction–like fashion all two hundred patients in the nursing home have cardiac arrest and die. The mischievous individual intended the prank; he in no way intended their deaths. Nor could he have reasonably foreseen even one death, let alone all two hundred, as a consequence of his prank. In other words, although he did what was wrong, and caused a great deal of harm in doing it, he did not act evilly.

Notice, by contrast, that a particularly hideous act (as characterized by the very nature of the act) often seems to have all the makings of evil. An adult who rapes a six-year-old is seen as having performed a hideous act. What inclines us to think so is that we suppose that a great many moral sensibilities must have been deadened in a person who rapes a six-year-old. In general, an evil act seems to be not only a wrongdoing, but a wrongdoing that evinces a profound deadening of moral sensibilities.

The law is useful here. It has allowed that there can be crimes of passion, and that a person can be so provoked to anger by another's words as to attack the other physically. Such allowed actions are hardly thought to be evil. On the contrary, precisely what the law allows is that there can be understandable reasons why a person is animated to harm another, aside from the person's having a morally reprehensible and foul character.

Revenge is even more interesting in this regard. The idea of getting back at another for a harm done, while often thought to be wrong, is rarely thought to be evil in and of itself. So understandable are feelings of revenge that it has been asked whether legal punishment itself is merely a form of institutionalized revenge. (There is the rather interesting phenomenon of what would seem to be group revenge, when the members of one group set out to revenge the harm that one of them has suffered from the members of another group. The individuals seeking revenge need not have been harmed at all. I shall not focus upon this phenomenon.)

The fact that crimes of passion and acts of revenge are generally not, in and of themselves, considered to be evil gives us a better fix on the nature of an evil act. There are understandable reasons for being animated by hostile feelings toward another. In fact, a person never so animated might very well give us pause. In instances of revenge, it is even understandable that a person takes delight in causing another harm; for revenge is said to be sweet. Thus, revenge tends to be rather unlike crimes of passion or the act of responding to fighting words, both being occasions when it is not readily presumed that a person takes delight in causing harm. Notice, though, that the deep satisfaction of revenge is supposed to be due not only to having caused harm but also to having evened the score, perhaps in a particularly clever and unsuspected way.

As a first approximation, then, an evil act may be regarded as a wrong act stemming from hostile feelings (on the part of a sane person) that are not animated by understandable factors. This description, of course, is not complete, since under these conditions acts such as inexplicable lies would too easily turn out to be evil. We often find it difficult to fathom why a person felt he had to lie, sometimes even persuading the liar of this as well; yet many lies, wrong and unfathomable though they may be, are not acts of evil. Here we can take a cue from the concluding remark about revenge in the preceding paragraph. An act is evil only if the agent both intends to harm and delights in harming the person in question, even if the agent has not in any way been harmed by the person. The suggestion here is not that, as a matter of conceptual truth, an act of revenge cannot also be evil, a point to which I shall return later. The point, instead, is that while revenge and evil share the feature of taking delight in causing another harm, evil differs from revenge in that evil does not require that one has been wronged by the person whom one is harming. By contrast, it is a conceptual matter that revenge requires this.

This brings us much closer to the truth in characterizing an evil act, but not quite close enough. Acts of petty theft illustrate this quite clearly. Imagine that a nurse takes a perverse delight in stealing small amounts of change from an elderly person. The nurse is clearly committing a wrong—and for inexplicable reasons, since he steals only enough change for a soda or candy. All the same, to regard this nurse's thievery from the elderly person as evil is surely to blow things out of proportion. An evil act must have a certain moral gravity to it. In this specific sense, evil acts are at one pole of a continuum that has acts of supererogation at the opposite end. Not every kind or thoughtful or beneficial or considerate thing a person might do counts as an act of supererogation, even if some degree of self-sacrifice is involved.[3] Only acts that have a certain moral gravity to them qualify as supererogation.

A person performs an evil act, then, if he delights in performing a harmful act that has a certain moral gravity to it (to be commented upon momentarily) and if the person is not animated by understandable considerations. Whereas normally a person's moral sensibilities would get in the way of his performing an act of such moral gravity, this does not happen when a person performs an evil act. On the contrary, the very gravity of

[3]As Lawrence Blum has masterfully shown in *Friendship, Altruism, and Morality* (New York: Routledge and Kegan Paul, 1980).

the act spurs him on. At any rate, these conditions are so in paradigm cases of acts of evil. If you will, an evil act must be a wrong act, done in the appropriate way, that has the right moral gravity to it. Thus, there is some justification for the claim that an evil act is rather like an Aristotelean virtuous act turned inside out; for Aristotle held that an act that is characteristic of a virtue such as honesty or courage must be done in the right way, for the right reason, and so forth. If one holds that neither children nor the insane are capable of performing evil acts, then one's account of such acts must be along these lines. It must be Aristotelian in the way indicated.

The above remarks easily apply to refrainings. A refraining is evil if it is done in the right way and has the right moral gravity to it. Suppose five babies are drowning in a wading pool on the lawn. The person merely strolling by, on her way to get an ice cream cone, need only unplug the pool's drain to prevent their deaths. It is inexplicable that she is not moved to do this. As the British moralist David Hume maintained, we expect morally decent persons to be pained by the manifest suffering of another, and to be moved to eliminate it if that can be done easily enough, as is so in our example. I shall not always stop to discuss the case of refrainings.

A harmful act is just that—one that causes harm. Nothing is gained by treating all harmful acts as evil acts. For, philosophically, we would still have to distinguish, among the class of evil acts, between intentional and nonintentional evil acts. And among intentional evil acts we would then need to distinguish between those that issue from delight in causing the harm of another and those that do not. And so on. By the time we finished our litany of distinctions, we would be mirroring the very distinction, between harmful and evil acts, that we had obliterated in the first place. This does not make for philosophical progress.

Regarding the moral-gravity condition, it is obviously a function of the hideousness of the act. However, there are two vectors of evil here: inherent hideousness and quantitative hideousness. These two vectors can operate together or independently of one another. We have an instance of the former in the rape of a six-year-old. We have an instance of the latter in the wanton murder of a hundred members of a community by a street gang out on a killing spree one night. Surely the hideousness of this second act is essentially a function of the number of people murdered: a hundred rather than only one person. If the gang killed one hundred people by skinning them alive, their actions would combine both inherent and quantitative hideousness. Or, the gang could do evil by killing even one person in a particularly gruesome and savage manner. The Holocaust and American Slavery combine both vectors of evil.

At this point, it might be objected that the notion of hideousness does not do much to explicate the idea of moral gravity. Furthermore, it might be noted that hideousness is surely in the eye of the beholder. As a response, it will be helpful to look briefly at the structure of acts of honesty and acts of courage. As we shall see, the structure of an evil act resembles that of a courageous act more than it does an honest deed.

For all practical purposes, an act of honesty is rigidly tied to a single well-defined behavioral component, namely telling the truth. There is not a host of behaviors that may or may not count as acts of honesty depending upon the circumstances. Thus an honest act is not person-relative in the way that courage is, in the sense of being dependent upon a person's makeup, what a person is used to doing, and the surrounding circumstances; although, to be sure, success at being honest is dependent upon these conditions. What counts as an act of honesty is generally undeniably clear, precisely because there is only one well-defined behavior, namely telling the truth, that counts. True, honesty includes refraining from stealing, which is not exactly the same as telling the truth; hence, it may be insisted that there are two well-defined acts that are components of honesty. Perhaps. Suffice it to say that a person who is honest with respect to truth telling is one who will not steal, which suggests that truth telling is dominant with respect to the virtue of honesty. A thief who always tells the truth, out of a deep and abiding love for truth, would make for a very bad thief. Perhaps we even have an incomprehensible description here, given the world as we know it.

Turning to courage, there is no single well-defined behavioral component to which an act of courage is rigidly tied. Although there are some acts that are characteristically thought to be courageous, courage is considerably person-relative. A differently abled person may display considerable courage in pursuing graduate training, whereas the average physically whole person does not. In a social setting where people are telling anti-Semitic jokes, it can be very courageous indeed to say that one is Jewish. By contrast, rarely would it be courageous to say in a face-to-face encounter that one is black or a woman, since these identities are usually evident. For a trained fire fighter, going into a burning building to save a life may not be nearly the courageous act that it is for a passerby, who knows nothing about fires in buildings except that they should be avoided but who risks her life anyway to save the person trapped inside. In fact, if courage is tied to overcoming fear, then a person trained in fire fighting may display no courage at all in going into the flames, since she may have very good reason to believe that, given the nature of the building and the character of the fire, she is in no danger of the building's collapsing in the next forty minutes or so. Yet, for all of this person-relativity, the notion of a courageous act hardly turns out to be meaningless. Nor does the concept of relativity apply in the repugnant sense in which the word has come to be used these days, meaning that courage is simply whatever a person takes it to be. One would have to tell an extraordinary story to turn yawning or wiggling one's nose into a courageous act or, on the other hand, to make a cowardly act out of jumping into the ocean to save a child threatened by a shark.

Likewise, although there are some acts that are characteristically thought to be evil, there is no single well-defined behavioral component to which an act of evil is inextricably tied. Gratuitous torture and other acts of cruelty come readily to mind as candidates for indisputably evil acts; yet, cruelty is not specific but ranges over a myriad of kinds of acts. American Slavery was cruel; the Nazi concentration camps were cruel. They were cruel in quite different ways, however. Rape is cruel; child abuse (whether physical or mental) is cruel. But, again, these practices are cruel in very different ways, both from one another and from the previous two examples of cruelty (even taking into account the institutional nature of the previous two examples). One can torture a person by killing each member of her family before her very eyes or by crudely pulling one tooth after another from her mouth. There is no need to continue. The point, I trust, is clear. And, of course, as with the virtues in general, behavior alone does not determine whether an act is evil. Neither torture nor the infliction of pain need, as a matter of logic, be gratuitous. Suppose it would take nothing short of torture to force an evil person to reveal the whereabouts of a thousand children destined to be killed or a thousand blacks destined for slavery in America. Torture would certainly be forgivable if done in the hopes of saving these lives from the horrific fate that awaited them.

Because evil, like courage, is not rigidly tied to a single well-defined act, the concept must be explicated in broad terms. We know that courage is a matter of facing certain kinds of danger, which may be a matter of overcoming certain kinds of obstacles (as with a handicapped person pursuing graduate work) in a certain kind of way. We know that evil is a matter of performing harmful acts of a certain moral gravity in a certain way. If, as we have clearly seen, the concept of a courageous act is hardly rendered meaningless on account of being defined in broad terms, then the concept of an evil act should not be rendered meaningless on that account alone, either. To be sure, whereas it takes only two broad categories to characterize a courageous act ("overcoming the fear of certain kinds of dangers in certain way"), it takes three to characterize an evil act ("performing harmful acts with a certain moral gravity in a certain way"). This difference should come as no surprise. Courage, after all, is but one virtue. Evil, on the other hand, is an inclusive notion.

From evil acts, I turn now to evil persons. My interest, though, is not really in offering a characterization of an evil person, as that should be straightforward enough given the preceding discussion of an evil act. An evil person or—as I prefer to say, for reasons that will soon become clear—a person with an evil character is one who is often enough prone to do evil acts. What I want to draw attention to, however, is that, first of all, there would not seem to be any sane person who is evil through and through, where this is understood to mean that there is no one toward whom the person would not act evilly. Second, it would be a mistake to suppose that a person either has an evil character throughout his adult life or not at all. An evil character can be a phase in a person's life, a trait that was clearly not there earlier on and from which the person may disassociate himself later. This raises a most interesting question, given my account of an evil act.

According to the account, a person can have an evil character only if he is lacking in certain sensibilities. The issue, of course, is how a person could have those sensibilities at one point but then lose them. The question takes on considerable force if, as I have claimed, there are no evil persons through and through. For then the question is this: How could a person not lacking in sensibilities toward anyone come to be lacking in sensibilities toward some but not others? Thus, in a most important respect, it is not the thoroughly evil person who is incomprehensible, except insofar as committing acts of evil is itself incomprehensible, but the person who is capable of genuine acts of evil toward some, and genuine feelings of caring toward others. It is this person, the morally bivalent person, as I shall say, who stretches to the very limits the human capacity for difference— nay, polarity. Essentially, the thoroughly evil person raises precisely the same problem that is in general raised by performing evil acts. The thoroughly evil person is the reiterated instance, in a single life, of the single case of evil. Insofar as we understand the single case, we will have a measure of understanding of the thoroughly evil person.

Not so with the morally bivalent person, however. We wonder how it is possible for the same life to exhibit such extremes, which conflict so explicitly and so radically. We wonder this because we assume a psychology of the self that would make it impossible for a sane self to handle extremes of explicit internal conflict without becoming an insane self, in which case the problem evaporates anyway. It is not inconsistency per se that we take to be the problem; for we know that people are capable of compartmentalizing, of holding inconsistent beliefs and values. This seems to be part of the psychological elasticity of the human condition, yielding both good and bad results. Cigarette smoking has become one of the classic examples of how this elasticity can be for the bad. This psychological elasticity is for the good, however, if only because we do not come by our beliefs and values all at once; nor, for that matter, do we always do so consciously. Not only that but different values speak to different concerns in our lives. We may simply not be prepared to give up two conflicting values, depending on how self-contained the conflict is.

This last point was illustrated earlier on in the case of the Orthodox Jewish feminist (Section 1).

A different illustration of the point: It has seemed to a great many black Americans that they should take greater pride in their African roots, throwing off the shame of black Africa that has been cultivated by Western culture. This objective seems laudable enough. There is tension here, however. On the one hand, a great many black Americans are steeped in the religious tradition of Christianity, a quintessentially Western religion. On the other, many quintessentially black African traditions not only predate Christianity, but are also somewhat at odds with Christianity—a religious tradition that, it can be plausibly argued, has played no small role in the denigrating attitude of Western culture toward African tradition in dance, music, and art. The conflict has been contained by focusing not so much upon the concomitant beliefs of past African traditions, but on the intricacies of the various rituals themselves: instead of primitive movements by simple people, we now have African dance as a sophisticated art form. The main concern has been not to be ashamed of African traditions as such. On the surface of things, the way in which the conflict between Christianity and African traditions has been contained would seem to be adequate; for the correctness of a tradition should not be a necessary condition for holding it in high regard. A tradition can be profoundly inspirational and insightful without being true, strictly speaking. Presumably, this is true of the Western philosophical tradition. I shall return to blacks and Christianity (Section 19).

With the morally bivalent person, however, the problem seems to be that there is no way in which the conflict owing to the extremes of good and evil in his life can be contained. How was it possible for Thomas Jefferson to be both the man of honor and integrity that he so clearly was and, at the very same time, a slaveholder—indeed, not just a slaveholder, but who one kept a slave as his mistress (Section 1). It is woefully unilluminating to say that human beings can compartmentalize, because precisely what is at issue is how it is possible for human beings to compartmentalize to that extent. Again, one wonders how it was possible for whites during American Slavery times to believe that a black woman made a most suitable nanny, with all that caring for a child implies in terms of providing moral guidance, yet believe also that the black woman was less than fully human, a point that I shall discuss more fully later (Section 16). Once more, it is outright unilluminating to say that human beings are capable of compartmentalizing. For one would think that if the humanity of anyone was to be acknowledged, it would be the humanity of those to whom one entrusted the well-being, both moral and physical, of one's children. After all, slaveowners did not experiment with child care by other living creatures—say, chimpanzees and dolphins—and only through trial and error settle upon black women for this role.

I have given two paradigm examples of moral bivalence during American Slavery. Nazi medical doctors are the paradigm example of moral bivalence during the Holocaust. I shall discuss the case of Nazi doctors in the next chapter.

I believe that one reason we have difficulty in understanding the phenomenon of moral bivalence is that we endeavor to do so on an individual level. That is, we want the explanation for any individual's moral bivalence to be limited to facts about the individual herself or himself, completely independent of the community to which the individual belongs. Perhaps we think that attributing moral responsibility requires such limits. I believe our discussion of Chambon (Section 7) shows that there is more to be said for community praise or blame than we are often inclined to suppose.

I remarked at the outset of the preceding chapter that a community is more than the sum of its members, and that a conviction, however strong, does not make a consensus. The moral consensus of a community can bear mightily upon how an individual behaves, both directly and indirectly—indirectly, by bearing upon the moral sensibilities to which we are susceptible. In making the latter point, I do not uphold the absurdly false claim that on no occasion can a person experience either guilt or shame except in the presence of others or unless others do like-wise. Rather, the idea is that our disposition to experience guilt and shame on account of wrongdoing cannot sustain itself, but needs reinforcement; and that reinforcement comes directly from the moral community with which a person basically identifies. First there is the cognitive recognition that one has performed a wrong act, then the experiencing of guilt and shame on account of doing so—the visceral experience, as we may call it. A moral community is key to there continually being a visceral experience or, at any rate, to that connection achieving a certain level of poignancy. In the language of social psychology, the moral com-munity with which a person basically identifies represents a moral audience; and a moral audience is a necessary condition for the continued visceral experiencing of guilt and shame.[4]

As one might imagine, though, the moral community with which a person basically identifies represents but one among many moral audiences that may exist for a person. This is so for a number of reasons. First of all, any society is likely to contain a multitude of moral communities, ranging from the saintly to the immoral. Second, a moral community is by its very nature a rather amorphous entity, which admits of pockets of varying de-grees of moral rectitude. Different kinds of moral communities can exist within city blocks of one another; and different moral communities of the same timbre may exist thousands of miles apart. In fact, a moral community can change by virtue of the label of the four walls of a building. We have one kind of moral community with a church, and a quite different kind with a por-nographic theater. A person may basically identify with one moral community but move among others in various ways, thus changing her or his moral audience.

[4]For the significance of a moral audience as I have used it in the text, I am much indebted to the collected essays in W. Ray Crozier (ed.), *Shyness and Em-barrassment: Perspectives from Social Psychology* (New York: Cambridge University Press, 1990).

To see just how much of a factor a moral audience is in a person's experience of guilt and shame on account of wrongdoing, consider the case of entering a pornographic theater. It is possible to feel quite ambivalent about entering such an establishment, and considerably less ambivalent after entering. This is no accident. Nor is the difference due merely to having taken the pornographic plunge, if you will, thereby undermining any doubts one might have had about viewing such a film. The most significant difference, actually, is the change in one's moral audience. Those seated inside the theater are indisputably voyeurs of pornography, whatever inclinations those on the outside might have. Any number of passersby on the street can represent the judgment that the right thing to do is to walk past the theater, that viewing pornographic movies is a morally despicable thing to do. Outsiders can point a moral finger of accusation, as it were. By contrast, it is with rare exception that anyone seated inside a pornographic theater could point in accusation. All who join the audience are (presumed to be) equally guilty.

Well, next to doing no wrong in the first place, nothing assuages the conscience like being in the company of fellow travelers in wrongdoing—the very same wrongdoing. Even if everyone is besieged with a profoundly pricked conscience, no one is able to take the moral high road with respect to anyone else. Hence, a patron is not confronted with the tension of having done what is wrong in the company of those who are innocent of that wrongdoing. Any reminder of the moviegoer's wrongdoing is not owing to the righteousness of his company.

Consider the difference between wrongdoing in complete privacy and wrongdoing that others witness. The latter is clearly more acute, if only because one's moral weakness is bared before others; in the former case, one can take comfort in the fact that no one knows. Ironically, however, wrongdoing in the company of others may sometimes provide even greater comfort, for then it can be said that others were not able to resist either. This gives a somewhat wicked twist to the thesis that there is safety in numbers. For not only can a number of people traveling together prevent physical harm to one another, they can also prevent one another entirely from experiencing guilt and shame on account of doing wrong, or at least lessen the intensity that each might have felt in isolation of one another.

If the above remarks are sound, they have two very significant, untoward implications. First of all, if one chooses moral audiences judiciously, taking care to keep some distance between conflicting moral audiences so that neither is aware of one's affiliation with the other, then it is possible to engage in dramatic wrongdoing without the visceral experience generated by awareness of the wrong. By choosing carefully the moral audiences among which one travels, one can be sure that no one is in the position to point a finger of moral accusation. The rest of the audience in the pornographic theater cannot do so; and the people in one's religious community would not even imagine that one visited such a den of iniquity. This is no doubt an unfortunate price we pay for the elasticity of the human mind. If a place of worship and a pornographic theater are located next door to one another, it would be very difficult indeed for the religious leader to leave the place of worship and enter the pornographic theater, as the two conflicting moral audiences would be too close for comfort; and the chances of being recognized in one audience as being affiliated with the other are far too great. In the proverbial small town, where everyone knows everyone else, any such move is difficult. However, in a densely populated metropolitan area, things are quite different. In such an area a person can very easily move from one audience to another without causing much internal conflict.

The second implication of our discussion is perhaps even more disconcerting: In any moral community, including one that professes moral rectitude, if enough people are known to commit the very same moral wrong, then visceral experiences with respect to that moral wrong are quite likely to evaporate, notwithstanding the cognitive recognition of the wrongness of the act. This is one highly significant upshot when a great many people, or a great many people of tremendous social standing, engage in an immoral activity or practice.

Let me return now to the morally bivalent person—that is, the person whose life exhibits both good and evil. It might seem that my account of the role of moral audiences has been too successful. For far from explaining moral bivalence, the account might appear to eliminate it altogether. Well, not exactly. While moral audiences are important, they are not decisive, regardless of circumstances. It is possible for a person both to have a moral audience that finds a certain form of behavior is acceptable and, at the same time, to have a range of concrete experiences that are manifestly at odds with the judgment of the moral audience. Thomas Jefferson's moral audience extolled the virtues of Slavery; his concrete experiences were manifestly at odds with the judgment of his moral audience. So it was, I suggest, for any slaveholder. Jefferson, of course, was no ordinary member of the moral community that constituted his moral audience. He was a founding member of the very society that he embraced. In social and political stature he was second to none. To an extent that is quite uncommon, Jefferson's standing in the community was not tied to how his behavior conformed to the standards of the community. As a result, his direct experiences with Slavery were somewhat morally tumultuous for him. He was able to acknowledge the voice of humanity in the experience of the slaves, even as he identified with the community that condemned blacks to less than human status. A person whose sense of self was more tied to measuring up to the standards of the community might have had more difficulty acknowledging the voice of humanity in the experiences of the slaves. The claim is not that the voice would have been less audible, but that the person might have had greater difficulty in acknowledging it. Indeed, the person might have taken steps to prevent against such an acknowledgment. One can drown out a voice. One can do things to people that make them seem less human. But just as flaunting a rule presupposes the very existence of that rule, so taking any steps to prevent the humanity of others from operating at a conscious level in one's life necessarily presupposes a recognition of their humanity. In the history of humankind, few groups of human beings have been subjected to systematic practices that denied, for the worse, the manifest reality of the group's biological category as human beings. It is much easier to engage in such denial in concert with others than alone.

But human beings are sui generis.[5] They are unique. Or, as I should prefer to say, human beings constitute a manifestly evident natural kind: There is a range of behavior that is characteristic of all biologically and psychologically healthy human beings exclusively, and it is manifestly evident as such to all like human beings. The closest to human beings known on the evolutionary scale are chimpanzees. In terms of their needs for affection, the parallels between human infants and chimpanzee infants are quite striking, but much greater differences separate adult human beings from adult chimpanzees. The object of any form of slavery has always been human beings. Likewise, the spoils of war in terms of sexual crimes have always been human beings, namely women. Were human beings readily confused with any other creature on earth, one would expect this confusion to show up in history. Warriors thinking they had captured human beings, say, would discover to their surprise that they had chimpanzees on their hands. This has never happened.

These remarks are not an aside. They underscore the point

[5]Here, I have been much inspired by Bernard Boxill's paper "Dignity, Slavery, and the Thirteenth Amendment," in Michael J. Meyer and W. A. Parent (eds.), *The Constitution of Rights* (Ithaca, N.Y.: Cornell University Press, 1992). He argues eloquently for the manifest obviousness of humanity, focusing particularly upon the case of black Slavery.

that human beings are a manifestly evident natural kind. Hence, any attempt to deny the humanity of any group requires significant and sustained psychological maneuvering. When persons who are morally upright in other respects of their lives aim to do this, we then have the conditions that make for moral bivalence. Given the assumption of biological and psychological health, any human beings who deny the humanity of others with whom they regularly interact are engaged in the attempt to live as true what is revealed to them as manifestly false by their most fundamental ongoing human experiences. It takes great effort to deny the ongoing reality of fundamental human experiences. It is only in the context of a community that any psychologically healthy human being has a chance at succeeding in doing so.

In the following chapter, I shall take a look at a special case of compartmentalizing whereby decent people are capable of performing both good and evil, namely the phenomenon of doubling that occurred in the concentration camps of Nazi Germany.

The Psychology of Doubling

9. The Problem

The notion of doubling in connection with the concentration camps was introduced by Robert J. Lifton in his book *The Nazi Doctors: Medical Killing and the Psychology of Genocide* (New York: Basic Books, 1986). The core idea is that there are two selves in the life of a single individual: a self of good and a self of evil. The words *two separate selves* are somewhat misleading. It is not that neither self knows what the other is doing. Rather, it is that a person's behavior is so baldly and significantly incongruous in an ongoing way in terms of displaying both good and evil behavior that one supposes that a person could live a life of such incongruity—could get on with her or his life in a meaningful way—only if the cognitive significance of the incongruity was ignored. Hence, a divided self. It is one thing to ignore a minor inconsistency, or one that can be suitably insulated, in one's life. No doubt everyone does that. But only individuals who are in some way divided can ignore that which is baldly and significantly incongruous in their lives. A person who believes that there are good moral reasons for not eating meat or not owning a luxury car may very well do so anyway. Or, as we saw (Section

1), a person may be deeply opposed to sexism, yet belong to an Orthodox synagogue, tolerating a preference given to men in Jewish religious ceremonies that would be utterly intolerable to her or him in almost any other context. Incongruities of this sort seem to be perfectly compatible with having a psychologically whole sense of self.

By contrast, it is extremely difficult to imagine that a person could devote his life to providing shelter for the homeless, be an off-and-on serial killer of children, and also have a psychologically whole personality. Lifton thinks of the Nazi medical doctors on this order. They belonged to and identified with a profession the defining aims of which were to save life, yet they explicitly and continually acted in ways that could not be more inimical to the very aims of their profession. Not only that, outside the confines of Auschwitz these individuals were often ordinary decent people. Lifton thinks that this constellation of circumstances does not make for a psychologically whole personality.

Lifton believes that five features are generally characteristic of the phenomenon of doubling (p. 419). (1) There is a "dialectic between two selves in terms of autonomy and connection." (2) "Doubling follows a holistic principle. The Auschwitz self 'succeeded' because it was inclusive and could connect with the entire Auschwitz environment." (3) "Doubling has a life-death dimension: the Auschwitz self was perceived by the perpetrator as a form of psychological survival in a death-dominated environment." (4) "A major function of doubling, as in Auschwitz, is likely to be the avoidance of guilt." (5) "Doubling involves . . . an unconscious dimension."

Berl Lang, in his important work, *Act and Idea in Nazi Genocide* (Chicago: University of Chicago Press, 1990), comments on Lifton's account of doubling, raising two objections. The first, which I shall call the practical objection, is this:

> The fact that the Nazi doctors or the camp guards might act differently in different "domains" does not mean, on this account, that

they are following different principles; the principles could be consistent or even identical, entailing differences in conduct because their "objects" are judged to differ. Such differences are common in other contexts; for example, the legal and the moral status of adults is distinguished from that of children with no implication that the principles underlying the differences are contradictory or even that they differ. (p. 53)

It is not, for example, that brutal medical experiments are conducted simply on children within the camp; but that the children who are the subjects of experiments have a designation which overrides their identity as children: they are Jews. This leaves the children who are not in the camp, the doctor's own children or others, as subject, not to the rules of a different moral world, but to the rules of the same one; they are treated differently not because of differences in the categories of two domains, but because children are categorized differently within the *same* domain. (p. 54)

There simply is no gainsaying Lang's formal point that differences in the treatment of different individuals hardly entail nonidentical or even incompatible principles. And again he is surely right in his observation that the children of the concentration camps were not only children; they were Jews.

The following is what I shall call the theoretical objection.

The divided self, so far as one can speak of it at all, is constructed by the self in order to avoid admitting what a unified self would have to—that is, the knowledge of the evil. That knowledge, however, is presupposed in the emergence of the divided self; it remains an ingredient in the two parts, furthermore, as they contrive to know each other with sufficient force and clarity to remain distinct. *Only* the knowledge of evil, it seems, would require a screen between the parts of the morally divided self that blocked out what would otherwise be openly present. (p. 56)

As one can see, the substance of this objection is that the very idea of a divided self is incoherent precisely because it presupposes the very thing whose existence it denies, namely a unified self. This objection would certainly seem to have an intuitive force to it. However, I believe that neither objection is well taken.

As to the practical objection: Surely it is implicit in the thought of almost anyone who writes in the hope of making some sense of the Holocaust that the designation "Jew" made all the difference in the world to the Nazis. It is precisely because the designation made such a difference that it cries out for an explanation. And how could individuals, otherwise committed to enhancing lives, participate in the brutal extermination of a people simply on account of their being Jewish? A description of what transpired here is crucial, and that is precisely what raises the specter of doubling.

Briefly, the Nazi doctors were not engaged in some project that had as its side effect the horrible death of many Jews, in the way that slave traders were engaged in the project of transporting slaves from Africa and were relatively indifferent to the horrible deaths that occurred along the way. No, the doctors were simply engaged in the project of exterminating a people, monstrous as it is to suppose that those who identified with a profession defined by saving life could nonetheless participate in the extermination of a people. It is one thing for medical doctors to be inured to the death of others when that is a side effect of their actions; it is quite another for them to be the agents of death, bent on exterminating a people. The inclusion of children makes the issue all the more poignant, for children generally exude an innocence that touches the hardest of hearts. Even slave children were granted a measure of dispensation, allowed to frolic with white children.

Viewed in this light, there does, indeed, seem to be an incredible tension between what the Nazi medical doctors professed to be and what they in fact did—a tension that it would be most unusual not to experience in an extremely disconcerting way.

And if the Nazi doctors did not feel that tension or, in any case, were not incapacitated by it, one should like to know how that was possible.

As to the theoretical objection, first a textual clarification: Lifton's account of doubling does not presuppose that those who doubled fail to know of their evil deeds. He tells us:

> In doubling, one part of the self "disavows" another part. What is repudiated is not reality itself—*the individual Nazi doctor was aware of what he was doing via the Auschwitz self* [emphasis added]—but the meaning of that reality. The Nazi doctor knew that he selected, but did not interpret selections as murder. One level of disavowal, then, was the Auschwitz self's altering of the meaning of murder; and on another, the repudiation by the original self of *anything* done by the Auschwitz self. From the moment of its formation, the Auschwitz self so violated the Nazi doctor's previous self-concept as to require more or less permanent disavowal. Indeed, disavowal was the life blood of the Auschwitz self. (p. 422)

The issue, then, is how it was possible for Nazi doctors to engage in such radical disavowals. This is not an issue for Lang because he is not convinced that such disavowing in fact occurred, writing:

> It cannot simply be assumed that the brutality of a Dr. Josef Mengele at Auschwitz or an "Ivan the Terrible" at Treblinka was left behind at the walls of the camps, that it would not also have been reflected in their lives outside of the walls—still less that there was such division in their actions within the camps. The burden of evidence, in fact, suggests the contrary. (p. 53)

For Lang, there is little reason to believe that any disavowing was required of Nazi doctors owing to a radical difference in their lifestyle within the walls of the camps versus their lifestyle outside those walls, since he thinks that a Mengele or an Ivan the Terrible might have been just as brutal outside the camps as they were within.

I do not wish to argue the historical facts on this issue. If they are on Lang's side, so be it. However, it is one thing to claim that the historical facts do not support the view that doubling occurred in the lives of Nazi doctors; it is another thing, altogether, to claim that, according to the best psychological theories available, doubling is not a psychological possibility for human beings. And clearly, the first premise cannot stand in for the second. If so, then the issue of understanding the phenomenon of doubling remains—and not just as an academic interest; for it seems implausible to suppose that the historical facts would universally show that doubling did not occur among the Nazi doctors. We should want to allow that some doubled, even if far fewer did than Lifton and others have been inclined to suppose. This would suffice to make doubling an important notion to understand.

There is one respect, however, in which I do agree with Lang; and this bring us to the task at hand. Lifton's account of doubling would not seem to be at all explanatory. That is, reflection upon the features that he takes to be generally characteristic of the phenomenon gives us little or no insight as to how the phenomenon could occur. What could precipitate the psychological state of doubling? A description of that state, no matter how rich, should not be taken for an explanation of how that state could occur. I want in what follows to make some progress with regard to the latter. I want to explain the phenomenon. I trust that it is not necessary to add that I have no desire to excuse Nazi doctors for the wrong that they did.

10. *Doubling and Multiple Personality Disorder*

An area of mental health that comes readily to mind when one reflects upon doubling is that of multiple personality disorder (MPD). In fact, both Lifton and Lang comment upon this disorder in their discussions of doubling. The third edition of the *Diagnostic and Statistical Manual of Mental Disorders* of the American Psychiatric Association gives the following criteria for MPD:[1]

(A) The existence within the individual of two or more distinct personalities or personality states (each with its own relatively enduring pattern of perceiving, relating to and thinking about the environment and one's self).

(B) Each of these personality states at some time, and recurrently, takes full control of the individual's behavior.

Both Lang and Lifton insist—and I certainly agree—that doubling is not an MPD. This is understandable enough because (1) having the psychic disorder of multiple personalities is involuntary, usually owing to a traumatic experience; (2) the switch from one personality to the other is usually a change that is triggered rather than brought about voluntarily, but in any case the host personality does not readily control the occurrence of the alter personalities; and (3) MPD persons are usually victims of some traumatic experience, often some form of abuse. If doubling were an MPD, then it would be, or come far too close for comfort to being, an excuse for the fulsome immoral behavior of the Nazi doctors, in whom the Auschwitz personality would be the alter personality. Clearly, that would not do. More ominous,

---

[1]The account of multiple personality disorder offered draws upon Frank W. Putnam, *Diagnosis and Treatment of Multiple Personality Disorder* (New York: Guilford Press, 1989); and Colin A. Ross, *Multiple Personality Disorder: Diagnosis, Clinical Features, and Treatment* (New York: John Wiley and Sons, 1989). For discussion of the role of sexual abuse in the formation of multiple personality disorder, see some of the vivid autobiographical popular accounts, e.g., James Frances Casey, *The Flock* (New York: Knopf, 1991) and Truddi Chase, *When Rabbit Howls: The Troops for Truddi Chase* (Jove, 1987). For more technical accounts of the role of sexual abuse, see Mick Hunter (ed.), *The Sexually Abused Male*, vol. 1, *Prevalence, Impact and Treatment* (Lexington, Mass.: Lexington Books, 1990).

though, it would seem to be morally offensive even to entertain the thought that Nazi doctors were victims, notwithstanding important works like Stanley Milgram's *Obedience to Authority* and Herbert C. Kelman and V. Lee Hamilton's *Crimes of Obedience*.[2] These works make it painfully clear that, often enough, ordinary people with quite acceptable moral ideals and aspirations far too readily acquiesce to institutional authority. This truth, sad as it may be, does not turn those who acquiesce into victims.

However, it is possible to be so eager to distance doubling from multiple personality disorders, lest one appear to be excusing the evil that was done, that one fails to notice important similarities. Particularly illuminating here is the formation of a multiple personality owing to childhood sexual abuse. Only one detail need be brought out, namely this: Out of fear of being either harmed or dismissed as fabricating malicious tales, the child feels that it cannot report the behavior to anyone.[3] Thus, the child must repeatedly endure in complete social silence an inconceivable agony. It cannot discuss the abuse it endures. It cannot discuss what has happened even if it has reason to believe that more than one adult in the house is aware of it. At any rate, so it is in cases that typically give rise to MPD.

It is one thing to be powerless to prevent a harm from being done to us; it is quite another not to be able to talk about that harm to anyone. The extent to which human beings are quintessentially social creatures is dramatically revealed by the fact that

[2]New York: Harper and Row, 1974, and New Haven: Yale University Press, 1989, respectively.

[3]See the important discussion of this by Martine Lamour, "Les abus sexuels a l'égard des jeunes enfants: séduction, culpabilité, and secret," in Marceline Gabel (ed.), *Les enfants victims d'abus sexuels* (Paris: Presses Universitaires de France, 1992). In *La violence impensable* (Paris: Nathan, 1991), Fredericque Gruyet et al. observe: "Or, l'enfant abusé a de nombreuses raisons de se taire: en premier lieu, il est soumis à la loi du silence qui règne dans sa famille. Il vit sous la constraint, si ce n'est 'sous terreur'" (p. 57).

social discourse about what is profoundly important to us, especially traumatic harms, is essential to our maintaining psychologically whole personalities. Thus, there is a deeper sense than one might have realized to David Hume's claim in *A Treatise of Human Nature* that the "minds of men are mirrors to one another's soul" (II.ii.5). Ideally, we need to share emotionally crippling experiences with others who will embrace us and respond to us with sympathy. At the very minimum, we need to be able to convey the depth of our wounds to at least one person who will *acknowledge* the damage that has been done to us. Or, if the nature of our circumstances is especially weighty, as when one must make a painful choice, we need to be able to convey this to at least one person who will *acknowledge* its weightiness. This is a condition of being psychologically whole.

Usually, this acknowledgment is forthcoming readily and immediately. But for most victims of sexual child abuse, this minimum condition is simply not met. It is extremely rare for a person to suffer a grave harm or to be faced with a weighty decision that is denied by almost everyone, especially those who are meaningful to the person. But this is exactly the plight of most children who are victims of sexual abuse. The child must endure complete social silence—that is, a complete nonacknowledgment of its suffering at the hands of another.

The formation of alter personalities, hence the development of MPD, is one of the ways in which the mind of the child copes with complete social silence in the face of continual sexual abuse.[4] In particular, the child often forms a personality whose function, if you will, is simply to cope with the abuse in the face of the reality of complete social silence. Significantly, though, social si-

---

[4] Ross, *Multiple Personality Disorder*, emphasizes that this is a very creative response on the part of children for coping with a devastating situation. See pp. 10–11, 76. The problem is that the strategy usually becomes self-defeating as time goes on.

lence does not mean that a third party does not know of the harm that a victim is enduring. It is the failure to put the matter into words that is particularly relevant here.

The relevance of the remarks in the preceding paragraphs to Auschwitz is this: There was the condition of complete social silence about the hideous moral atrocities that were being committed against the Jews. People knew; people suspected. But one could not publicly question the morality of what was being done to the Jews—or even voice one's suspicions—without jeopardizing one's very life: One could not do so within the camps; one could not do so outside the camps. The moral weightiness of the situation was not a matter to be discussed. Specifically, it was not possible for Nazi medical doctors to avow, and to have others acknowledge, their abhorrent deeds as Nazi doctors—at least not without risking their lives. These remarks, for all of the awkwardness they may cause in reflecting upon them, are true nonetheless. As I shall make plain later, however, this truth does not in any way excuse what the Nazi doctors did. I am interested here only in making salient the parallel between the social circumstances of typical cases of MPD owing to child abuse and the social circumstances surrounding Nazi doctors—namely what I have called the phenomenon of social silence.[5]

To be a Nazi medical doctor was to engage in an extraordinary range of behavior, far beyond anything to which one could have been remotely accustomed, without being able to engage with another in any open moral reflection whatsoever about the character of one's deeds. Specifically, one could not display any sign of moral objection to what was being done. All the usual feelings of moral horror that might naturally be called forth when killing and witnessing the killing of innocent people, espe-

---

[5]I have profited considerably from Bruno Bettelheim's essay "Remarks on the Psychological Appeal of Totalitarianism," in his *Surviving and Other Essays* (New York: Alfred A. Knopf, 1979).

cially children, had to be suppressed, lest their display be taken not simply as a sign of weakness, which was risky enough, but as a sign of disapproval, which sufficed to put one's life in jeopardy.

Whatever else one did in Auschwitz one did not express moral disapproval of the horrors that were being perpetrated against the Jews. One did not do so even if one made it clear that one lacked the psychic wherewithal to perform such tasks of horror oneself. And, obviously, what one did in Auschwitz was not to be discussed with anyone outside the camps. Thus, the time spent away from the camps was not an opportunity to get one's moral bearings, as it were. One could not allow whatever feelings of moral horror that one had suppressed within the walls of the camps to be displayed outside those walls—at least not without putting one's life in jeopardy. For the Nazi regime did not tolerate disapproval, no matter where it was expressed.

Recall at this point Lifton's observation: "From the moment of its formation, the Auschwitz self so violated the Nazi doctor's previous self-concept as to require more or less permanent disavowal. Indeed, disavowal was the life blood of the Auschwitz self."

11. *The Psychology of Doubling*

Thanks to our brief discussion of sexual child abuse, we are in a position to shed some light on Lifton's remarks. Nazi Germany has the unenviable distinction of having been able to impose what for all practical purposes was complete social silence across an entire land with regard to the atrocities of the concentration camps. It did so, obviously, by threatening death. People were afraid to breathe even a word of disapproval. But, of course, the vast majority of people took no direct part in the atrocities committed against the Jews in the concentration camps. However much people might have approved of what was done, and however loathsome we might rightly find them for doing so, their approving of such atrocities is a far cry from their committing those atrocities themselves. The vast majority of people did not have to become inured to killing hundreds upon hundreds on a daily basis. And even if they thought they could do so, they never had to find out.

But how is it possible to ignore or discount the moral significance of killing hundreds upon hundreds of people on a daily basis? Part of the explanation most certainly has to do with the social silence that was imposed.

Consider a case of not being able to reflect openly about an unusual, but nonetheless trivial, act committed by one's own hands. Suppose, for example, that a group of people were required to unwrap ordinary tape from around thousands upon thousands of drinking glasses that appeared to be in excellent condition and then to wrap new, but otherwise ordinary, tape around them again and, moreover, suppose that the people were ordered, on pain of death, not to make any comments, except for approval, about the matter to anyone. To be sure, the order of silence itself would give some significance to a seemingly meaningless task. The people who handled the glasses would understandably be puzzled by an order of absolute silence with regard to such a trivial task. And speculation would no doubt abound. All the same, there is nothing negative in the nature of the task itself. Even if we allow that the task is rather insulting to everyone with even a measure of talent, it must be conceded that the moral character of the task is unassailable, accept insofar as there is something morally objectionable in requiring people of talent to perform meaningless tasks. But this criticism, sound though it might be, hardly shows that the task is morally objectionable—certainly not inherently so. No matter how difficult it might be for people to put up with such an intellectually unrewarding task, surely no one would lose sleep over it on moral grounds.

To be sure, individuals in the group would be open to the criticism that they had deceived others relentlessly as to the importance of their deeds. But no one would have to be concerned that the true fulsome character of their secret deeds would be discovered, since by hypothesis their deeds are not morally repugnant. Hence, although their living a lie must itself be countenanced as an immorality, the immorality of their living a lie would not be masking yet another ongoing immorality—certainly not an ongoing immorality of a much greater magnitude. Thus, while it would be natural for the members of the group to experience some cognitive dissonance owing to the disparity between their account of their task and the nature of that task, there simply would not be the possibility of others' discovering that the members of the group were capable of a range of immoral behavior completely out of step with their public personae, which very few people would have had the wherewithal to perform. Most significantly, our imagined glass tapers would not have to come to grips with publicly masking highly immoral behavior that was an ongoing part of their lives, the threat of silence notwithstanding. Thus, in Lifton's terminology, no moral disavowals would be necessary.

Not so with the many Nazi doctors. Now, as Lang rightly reminds us, there can be no doubt that some Nazi doctors took a perverse delight in killing Jews. But we need not suppose either that all Nazi doctors doubled or that none did. Nor need we suppose that every Nazi doctor who came to the camps did so with the hope of being able to kill thousands upon thousands of Jews daily. We need not suppose that doing so was relished from the very start. And if the idea was relished in the abstract, there is lots of evidence that putting the idea into practice was more difficult to handle psychologically than was first thought. Thus, the gas chambers were not only more efficient as a means of killing Jews; they also made the task of doing so much easier to handle psychologically than using guns to kill thousands upon thousands of Jews on a routine basis.

Of course, it goes without saying that if every Nazi doctor had been entirely immune to the humanity of the Jews, then it would be very difficult, indeed, to make a case for the phenomenon of doubling. In this sense, Lang is absolutely right. If we are to suppose that Nazi doctors were evil persons *tout court*, then the very idea of doubling becomes rather empty. But Lang failed to appreciate the significance of his own words. To put the matter somewhat rhetorically, the thoroughly evil person would just as soon kill his very own parents or children if they got in the way of his aims. And while this may be true of some Nazi doctors, it would not seem to be true of all of them. Adolph Eichmann himself had his affections, so it would seem, and for a Jew, no less.[6]

The phenomenon of doubling arises precisely in those instances when it was impossible for a Nazi doctor to escape the tug of the humanity of the Jews, and P. F. Strawson has masterfully shown that entirely escaping the humanity of a person is much more easily said than done.[7]

One of Strawson's fundamental claims is that, cases of anthropomorphizing aside, only human beings can be an object of our resentment. We do not resent trees or cats or cars, though we can certainly be angry at any of them. It is a conceptual matter that resentment takes as its object only whatever is capable of agency, and it is conceptually impossible to resent what we believe has no agency. And alas, however inherently evil the Jews may have been according to the Nazis, it is inescapable that the Nazis believed the Jews to be capable of human agency. The

---

[6]In her book *Eichmann in Jerusalem* (New York: Penguin, 1964), Hannah Arendt writes: "It seems that in Vienna, where [Eichmann] was so extraordinarily successful in arranging the 'forced emigration' of Jews, he had a Jewish mistress, an 'old flame' from Linz" (p. 30).

[7]"Freedom and Resentment," *Freedom and Resentment and Other Essays* (London: Methuen, 1974). These remarks in the text are a response, if only an oblique and incomplete one, to the very challenging work of Susan Wolf, *Freedom Within Reason* (New York: Oxford University Press, 1990).

enormous display of resentment that Nazis exhibited toward Jews belies any claim that the Nazi death camps so undermined the humanity of the Jews that its presence could no longer be felt by the Nazis. As I have said (Section 8), human beings constitute a manifestly evident natural kind. I believe that Lifton subscribes, albeit unwittingly, to Strawson's position.

When Strawson's insight is combined with the observation that I have made concerning evil and social silence, I think that Lifton's idea of doubling survives critical scrutiny. Doubling occurs when people have to disavow the profound moral reality of the horror of their deeds owing to the condition of imposed social silence. Some Nazi doctors were never able to escape the tug of humanity that is a deeply rooted part of all human beings capable of agency. Yet, the activity of routinely killing large numbers of Jews on a daily basis requires that one be inured to their humanity. Any Nazi doctor who participated in the selections for death, but who could not escape the tug of the humanity of the Jews, had to mask the evil of his deeds given the condition of social silence that was imposed. Indeed, once having participated in the selections, a Nazi doctor could not cite moral grounds in refusing to repeat his actions; he could at best claim that he lacked the psychological wherewithal to do so. Recall the discussion in Section 4 on becoming morally sullied.

I suggest that the sort of public masking behavior alluded to earlier is what made it possible for those Nazi doctors who participated in the selections to ignore the humanity of the Jews just enough to be able to send Jews to their death. More precisely, I suggest that the public masking behavior that the Nazi doctors engaged in made it possible for those doctors who could not escape the humanity of the Jews not to feel the full cognitive significance in recognizing that humanity. The public masking made it possible for such Nazi doctors to engage in acts of disavowal.

So we do indeed have an explanation for two different sorts of moral behavior. By hypothesis, the public masking entailed a form of self-presentation to others that denied the horrible reality of one's immoral behavior in the camps. On the other hand, in the camps one engaged in a most evil sort of harming of others the cognitive significance of which one was able to minimize. This looks very much like what Lifton calls doubling.

One more observation is in order here. Extreme social silence over time minimizes, or eliminates entirely, the conditions for embarrassment.[8] Owing to the imposed social silence, the possibility of moral embarrassment for the murdering of thousands upon thousands of Jews was virtually eliminated in the camps. And this, too, helped make it possible for Nazi doctors to disavow any tug of the humanity of the Jews.

I do not deny Lang's profound observation that the Nazi doctors chose to do evil. We differ in how we fill out this story of choice. For one thing, there can be no doubt that many had ideological commitments that put them upon a slippery moral slope. There is no need to deny this. Nor is there any need to deny that many were in principle committed to killing the Jews. But this truth does not rule out the possibility of doubling. One might either lack the wherewithal to realize a commitment or find that realizing it affects one in unanticipated ways. Some Nazi doctors were so committed to the extermination of the Jews that the humanity of the Jews barely registered. There is no reason to suppose that all Nazi doctors were so committed to extermination. Doubling could occur if there were at least some for whom the selections were more of a moral challenge than anticipated.

Lifton tells the story of Dr. Ernst B., a committed Nazi who, according to Lifton, remained committed to Nazi ideology many years after the Holocaust. Yet, despite Dr. B.'s commitment to Nazi ideology, he did not participate in the selections of victims. Indeed, not only was this the case, but Dr. B. was, as an

---

[8]I am indebted here to the collection of essays by W. R. Crozier, *Shyness and Embarrassment: Perspectives from Social Psychology* (New York: Cambridge University Press, 1990).

Auschwitz doctor, so kind to Jews that their testimony on his behalf won his acquittal (ch. 16). He was called "a human being in an SS uniform" (p. 303). And Ernst B. is among those Nazi doctors who, according to Lifton, doubled—albeit not to the extent of others.

I should not want to excuse any Nazi doctor who participated in the death selections. If we allow that they simply made a choice for evil, as Lang wishes to do, then surely there can be no excusing them. I do not believe that the phenomenon of doubling excuses them, either. For as Aristotle observed, we can be responsible for the moral morass in which we become entangled. We can see this clearly in a traffic fatality owing to driving in an intoxicated state. More and more, such deaths are considered instances of first-degree murder. Intoxication does not excuse the driver who voluntarily puts herself in that drunken state; no one can claim to be ignorant of the fact that drunkenness causes incompetent driving, and a person has a deep and abiding moral obligation not to put herself in a psychological state in which she engages in reckless behavior with respect to the lives of others.

If in the morning Jones knowingly and voluntarily puts herself in a position that will lead her to harm Smith badly by afternoon, there can be no question that Jones bears significant moral responsibility for the harm that she causes Smith even if, at the moment of harming Smith, Jones does not fully apprehend the nature of her deeds. It is an important part of moral responsibility that we be mindful of the foreseeable consequences of our actions, and that we not render ourselves oblivious to our harming others.

12. *Moral Disassociation*

Why is it that the account of doubling, or in any case the amplification of Lifton's account, does not excuse those Nazi medical doctors who doubled? First of all, let me distinguish the term *disassociation*, as I am using it, from *dissociation*. In psychology, the latter refers to the idea of compartmentalizing.[9] By the former I mean discontinuing one's association with an activity or practice.

Let me observe that, as often as we think of doing so, opposing evil institutions requires considerable moral courage. The idea seems to be that a person should be prepared to face death or at least considerable harm to himself or his loved ones, perhaps both. I dare say that it will not come as a surprise to anyone that most people simply are not that courageous. Nor is it obvious to me that people are open to moral blame on account of not being so morally courageous. Clearly, not many people had the courage of Raoul Wallenberg, and no moral criticism of them is intended.

I suggest, then, that if we maintain that the Nazi doctors are open to grave moral blame, we would do well not to insist that this is so because they lacked the courage of a saint or a hero; for this is too high a moral standard to invoke. Not only that, but as one Holocaust survivor pointedly reminded me, it is to trivialize the power of fear of death as a motivating factor with respect to securing compliance behavior. And Hitler used fear masterfully. I suggest that we look, instead, at the moral significance of moral disassociation.

Moral disassociation can often be a form of moral resistance, achieved with a minimal amount of effort. Sometimes it is simply a matter of doing nothing. Sometimes it is a matter of failing to exhibit with competence any of the behavior that is required. It can be a masterful way of not doing what one has been ordered to do. Most significantly, moral disassociation does not

[9]See Jerome L. Singer (ed.), *Repression and Dissociation* (Chicago: University of Chicago Press, 1990), and Martha Heineman Pieper and William Joseph Pieper, *Intrapsychic Humanism: An Introduction to a Comprehensive Psychology and Philosophy of Mind* (Chicago: Falcon II Press, 1990).

require that one in any way criticize the practice in question. Thus, while moral disassociation may very well require courage, it does not usually require extraordinary courage. What is more, nor does moral disassociation require that one have standing or leverage with those of whose behavior one disapproves. Individuals often lack the wherewithal to criticize their superiors, and there are obvious risks in doing so. Hence, it is clear why criticizing one's superiors can often be a matter of considerable moral courage.

The beauty of moral disassociation, however, is that it requires no leverage whatsoever with one's superiors. Not only that, while it is well-nigh impossible to criticize another, morally or otherwise, without that person's realizing it almost immediately, one can easily engage in moral disassociative behavior without it being apparent that one is morally critical of the practice in question—if only because moral disassociative behavior, by its very nature, does not announce itself as that in the first place. I suggest, then, that the failure to disassociate morally from wrongdoing is rarely if ever excusable, as this tactic can almost always be used with ingenuity and cleverness sufficient to mask any disapproval of the practice in question. As one should surmise, I further suggest that moral disassociating from wrongdoing is a deep, all but inescapable, obligation on the part of each individual. On the one hand, I want to concede that it is perhaps too much to expect the ordinary citizen to have the courage to stand up to evil practices. On the other, though, I want to insist that the unwillingness to disassociate from evil practices constitutes a deep moral failing. *This is the moral failing of which I accuse the Nazi doctors.* We can allow our moral characters to become so sullied that we no longer have the wherewithal to engage in moral disassociation from what we recognize to be wrong—nay, so sullied that we become inured to the suffering of others, even at our own hand. The Nazi doctors, insofar as they doubled, are guilty of this moral failing. For it will be remembered that it is a consequence of Lifton's account that, had not the humanity of the Jews had some pull for these doctors, they would not have doubled in the first place.

It may be objected that moral disassociation alone is an inadequate response. Each Nazi doctor had a moral obligation to do more than that. Each had an obligation to try to persuade others of the moral atrociousness of the Nazi camps. There can, in fact, be no doubt that one can always do more than disassociate morally from wrongdoing. It is far from clear, though, that a further response can always be reasonably expected. Surely, there must be some circumstances when moral disassociation is the best that one could reasonably hope for, however much room there might be left for acts of heroism. It seems to me that if Auschwitz does not constitute a case in point, then nothing does. A measure of moral disassociation on the part of many would have gone a long way toward undermining the ends of Auschwitz.

I conclude with two observations. First, although Lifton tells us that Ernst B. doubled to some extent, it is clear that Ernst B. also engaged in moral disassociative behavior with respect to selections of victims. Most notably, he did not participate in the selections. He even managed to be kind to Jews on a routine basis, though not necessarily in an ostentatious manner. Second, there can be little doubt that had more Nazi doctors engaged in disassociative behavior only to the extent that Ernst B. did, things would gone very differently for the Jews of those years. And if this is true, then it is clear that a little disassociation from evil practices on the part of a great many individuals can go a mighty long way toward undermining the aims of evil itself. The Nazi doctors are to be faulted for not having done so. The hope is that a like fault does not lie within our own lives.

Some final remarks: Evil is opportunistic. It can make do with only a small crack in the armor of moral decency. Along this line, nothing serves evil better than initial ambivalence. For one thing, hesitation in the face of evil can undermine one's moral leverage. Recall our discussion about becoming morally sullied (Section 4). A person who does not object to a wrongdoing when it first occurs is, on that account alone, often in weaker position to object should the wrongdoing be repeated. An excuse for going along with what is proposed can be as simple as the fact that one did so yesterday. For another, the hesitation of ambivalence can also render one more susceptible to peer pressure. We often try to persuade people to join in. But, other things equal, we are far more likely to attempt to persuade the person who is wavering than the person who is adamant that she will have no part of the activity in question. This is hardly surprising. We run the risk of being disrespectful of a person's feelings and wishes when we try to persuade her to do what she is unwaveringly set against doing. Not so in the case of a person who is wavering. Third, and most significant, sometimes all it takes is sensing ambivalence on the part of others to give a person the feeling that he can get away with a certain kind of behavior, as surely every parent knows.

When Hitler came to power, he did not immediately begin exterminating the Jews. He first introduced euthanasia programs, which did not specifically target Jews, but the infirm. There was much ambivalence among the citizens about this. Even had there been strong opposition to the euthanasia programs, the Holocaust might still have occurred. But it is one thing to move from a tolerated public policy of killing the infirm, whoever they turn out to be, to a program of exterminating a people said to be evil. It is quite another matter to move from a public policy of respecting the life of all to a program of exterminating an entire people. The former requires only a slide, a "mere" shift in policy direction; the latter requires a fundamental leap from one set of values to a contrary set. Hitler did not have to leap. A little ambivalence can go a long way toward the realization of enormous amounts of evil. Clear indifference is often a veritable launching pad for evil. Recall our remarks about the Evian Conference (Section 5).

This is the last chapter of Part I. There is a moral to the arguments of these chapters. I can best get at it with a few sentences about the parent-child relationship.

For the most part, a single instance when parents say to their child "I love you" and kiss and hug the child is insignificant in itself. In general, no single instance will make the difference in a child's being secure in its relationship with its parents, and going on to be a secure adult. But twenty years of such instances constitute a tidal wave of affirmation for which there can be no substitute. Indeed, no array of hugs and kisses at age twenty or thirty can begin to make up for their absence during one's childhood. Being psychologically secure, when this is tied to parental love, is not owing to some momentous event of parental affirmation, but to the sustained small instances of affirmation that are forthcoming in one's childhood whether or not one wants or needs them.

Here, then, is the relevance to evil. Evil does not occur in a vacuum, especially wholesale evil against a people. It invariably starts with a crack in the community armor of moral goodness. And while one person alone may make a difference for the better, there can be no substitute for the collective resolve and steadfastness of a people against evil. Thus, the answer to how wholesale evil against a people can occur is not to be found in some metaphysical realm, but rather in the moral character of the communities to which we belong and with which we identify. Widespread ambivalence or indifference in a community resounds, creating a tonal quality, if you will, that emboldens evil.

PART II

The Institutions

American Slavery
and the Holocaust

I shall focus upon two ways in which American Slavery and the Holocaust were fundamentally different from one another. I shall begin with an account of the conception that each institution had of its victims. Then I shall examine the way in which each institution treated its victims. As one would imagine, the conception that each institution had of its victims is most relevant here. A third difference to be discussed concerns what I call natal alienation, which I shall take up in the following chapter.

The account that follows is not meant to be an indictment of every German or every white who lived in the environment of either Nazi Germany or American Slavery. It is manifestly false that every such German or American white viewed Jews and blacks, respectively, in the ways that I shall specify. Further, in some instances, at least, there was undoubtedly ambivalence on the part of those whose behavior was quite morally reproachable. I hardly intend to deny any of this. Rather, I am interested in capturing the kinds of considerations that were a part of the evil moral climate of the two oppressive institutions and that were embraced to varying degrees by the members of the societies in question.

Similarly, there can be no doubt that not every black or Jew was treated in the ways that I shall describe. But the measure of a moral climate is not found in its exceptions. An evil society is no less evil if it fails to abuse every member of the class of persons treated evilly, any more than a just society is any less that because of occasional miscarriages of justice.

13. *The Conception of the Victims*

Slavery did not have its inception in the United States. The Apostle Paul had nothing like American Slavery in mind when he intoned, "Servants, be obedient to them that are your masters" (Ephesians 6:5). However, it is in the United States that slavery took its most pernicious form. And it is about as self-evident as things get to be in the world of facts that skin pigmentation made a most dramatic difference in the pernicious turn that slavery took in the United States; for it allowed biology to serve as a manifest criterion of difference, obviating any social adornment. One could see that a person was black—or white—regardless of the manner of speech or dress. In theory, the problem of misidentification of status could not arise. In this respect, skin color was vastly better than social pedigree, which was ineluctably a matter of social adornment. Besides, the United States, being a nascent nation, had no history of social pedigree to moderate things. In the throes of forging its own identity, the United States was ripe for pernicious slavery, more so than Western European nations at the time. Pernicious slavery satisfied the twin ideals of equality and superiority: All whites got to be equal to one another, in theory at least; and all got to be superior to blacks, in fact. Western European nations already had too long a history of deep social stratification for pernicious slavery to yield the same results there.

Now, unlike human feelings of superiority based upon divine

right or pedigree, those based upon differences supposedly given by nature require that the object of contrast be of the right sort. It is true, that human beings are intellectually superior to cows, say, but the comparison is quite uninteresting. Human feelings of superiority require that the contrasting object be capable of imitating some of the excellences in which the superiority consists. Usually this means that the contrasting object must be seen as capable of some, but never complete, development with respect to the excellences that define the superiority.

I believe that the term that best characterizes the attitude of slaveowners toward slaves in the United States is that of moral simpleton; for although it implies that slaves in general are not able to make the grade, it also allows that they can have a sense of their own inadequacy. One does not imagine that cows might have any sense of their own inadequacy vis-à-vis human beings. The notion of moral simpleton is compatible with a paternalistic attitude toward blacks, but does not entail having such a posture. It is compatible with blacks being lazy, but does not entail shiftlessness, as the image of Sambo does. Notwithstanding the nefariousness of American Slavery, there can be no denying that a rich array of emotions passed between slaves and slaveowners, ranging from utter contempt on the part of slaveowners to undeniable feelings of outright affection between the two. The notion of moral simpleton is compatible with this fact. Just as adults can love children who cannot attain the full measure of any human excellence, so also can adults love moral simpletons who are incapable of any human excellence in full measure. Finally, the notion is elastic enough to allow for slaves to have a wide range of responsibilities, as it has never been the case that only the fully mature—that is, those who are both intellectually and morally mature—are capable of shouldering any significant responsibility. Teenagers, for example, are often given a wide range of quite significant responsibilities, including caring for their siblings, though no one supposes that in general teenagers are fully mature.

Offhand, the notion of moral simpleton perhaps seems incompatible with the widespread sexual exploitation of blacks, as well as sexual liaisons between white slaveowner and black female slave that were rich in genuine affection. Indeed, the liasions were often rich enough to arouse considerable jealousy in slaveowners' wives. On this matter, here are the words of Harriet Jacobs, who was born a slave but became a free person:

> Every where the years bring to all enough of sin and sorrow; but in slavery the very dawn of life is darkened by these shadows. Even the little child, who is accustomed to wait on her mistress and her children, will learn, before she is twelve years old, why it is that her mistress hates such and such a one among the slaves. Perhaps the child's own mother is among those hated ones. She [the child] listens to violent outbreaks of jealous passion, and cannot help understanding what is the cause. She will become prematurely knowing in evil things. Soon she will learn to tremble when she hears her master's footfall. She will be compelled to realize that she is no longer a child. If [the Almighty] has bestowed beauty upon her, it will prove her greatest curse.[1]

It would appear that if slaveowners insisted on the status of black slaves as moral simpletons and, at the same time, took slaves for their sexual pleasure, the slaveowners would be engaging in acts of perversion by their own lights. What prevents this supposition from being a telling objection is the existence of sexism itself; for it is the sexual exploitation of black women that was most prevalent. The world of American Slavery was also a world rife with sexism. Though much was made of protecting the honor of white women against black men, it must be remembered that in general white women on their own had very little standing in American society. Undeniably, there was a community consensus that placed some constraints on what a white

---

[1]Harriet Jacobs, *Incidents in the Life of a Slave Girl* (1861; New York: Oxford University Press, 1988). pp. 45–46.

man could do to a white woman, including his wife, and virtually none on what a white man could do to a black woman.
Still, it must be remembered that by no means were women full-
fledged members of society. This truth was not lost on some
white women who believed that the supposedly wide social distance between themselves and slaves was at times more apparent
than real. Mary Chesnut (ca. 1840) asserted: "There is no slave,
after all, like a wife."[2] This is revealing, even if an exaggeration.

White women were thought to be incapable of the full intellectual maturity and the moral depth of white men, although
there were virtues, such as compassion, that women were thought
to possess to a far greater extent than men. My point is that,
quite aside from slavery, the world of sexism sanctioned men's
sexual involvement with human beings who were said, by men,
not to be capable of full maturity. So it could hardly make a
dramatic difference in terms of sexual mores per se if the human
beings involved should be not only a bit more lacking in maturity but should also turn out to be black. To be sure, it was
possible for some wives of slaveowners to believe that black slave
women corrupted the morals of white men, either by tempting
them or by always being at the forcible disposal of white men.
But what is at the heart of this objection is marital fidelity rather
than the skin color of the persons with whom the husbands were
having sexual intercourse.

I do not suppose that the existence of sexism entirely explains
the sexual exploitation of blacks. Surely there were other relevant
factors. I have drawn attention to sexism, however, because the
prevalence of sexism made it a normal way of life for men to
have sexual relations with those who were (supposedly) inferior
to them. Accordingly, the mere inferiority of black women to

[2]As quoted in Elizabeth Fox-Genovese, *Within the Plantation Household: Black
and White Women of the Old South* (Chapel Hill: University of North Carolina
Press, 1988), p. 359.

white men could hardly have given white men pause in a sexual context.

The term moral simpleton, then, would seem to withstand critical scrutiny in terms of the prevailing practices of American Slavery. I have chosen the term for another reason as well.

I believe that the term moral simpleton accords well with the place that blacks have been traditionally understood to have in Western culture, which is essentially no place at all. I am not interested in debating the efforts of some to show that Greek thought as represented by Plato and Aristotle has its roots in Africa. Nor do I wish to debate whether early Egyptian thought is properly considered African thought. My point is that at the time of American Slavery, Africa was not thought to have had a central role in the history of moral and intellectual Western thought—not even, in fact, the role of a substantial footnote. Likewise for Africa with respect to Christianity, one of the cornerstones of Western thought. It was believed that only a people made up of moral simpletons could have been so lacking in contributions to the development of humankind.

Finally, I believe that the idea of moral simpleton fits well with the stereotype of blacks in America, and perhaps the world, today. The physical prowess of blacks has never been denied. Nor has the ability of blacks to excel at singing and at so-called popular forms of dance. These attributes notwithstanding, the moral and intellectual contributions of blacks, taken as a people, remain extremely marginal in the minds of many.

I turn now to the conception of the Jews during the Holocaust. To begin with, Jews have a secure place in Western thought. This accomplishment has been assured by Christianity itself, since it was in the womb of Judaism that Christianity is thought to have been conceived. Ironically, having a secure place in Western culture has not served Jewish people well. For, so the narrative goes, Judaism gave birth to the salvation of the world, and then had the temerity to reject it. To reject a good is one thing; to reject the very good that one produced is quite another. The narrative insists that Jews did the latter, killing the very bearer of world salvation, namely Christ himself. The Jews have an unenviable claim on being both the most famous and the most infamous people of Western culture.

It is very important to appreciate the source of the infamy of the Jews. It is not only that they are said to have killed Christ. In the New Testament, particularly the Gospel of St. John, the Jews are portrayed as explicitly rejecting that which is manifestly good. On various occasions, Christ is reported to have said to Jews that if the good deeds he had done before them had been done in Sodom and Gomorrah, the people there would long since have repented. The Jews to whom Christ was speaking are inevitably portrayed as finding some fault or other with what he did.

More important, in the Gospel of St. John, Christ reportedly accuses the Jews of having the devil himself as their father (John 8: 42–47). It does not take much to appreciate the implications. The story has it that the devil—Satan—is not only evil but irredeemably evil. It is Satan who, as the angel of Lucifer, attempted to overthrow God. We have here an explicit rejection of that which is manifestly good. As it is with Satan, so it is with Jews. The conception of the Jews that prevailed during the Holocaust and that is characteristic of anti-Semitism in general is that of being irredeemably evil. It took an especially virulent form during the Holocaust.

This conception of the Jews is not only compatible with but is in fact the explanation of many of the absurd hostile beliefs that people have had about Jews, such as holding that they used the blood of children in commemorating the Passover.[3] The stereotype of the Jew, which persists to this day, is that of a sly, greedy

[3]For a seminal discussion of anti-Semitism, see two Gavin I. Langmuir works: *History, Religion, and Antisemitism* (Los Angeles: University of California Press, 1990) and *Toward a Definition of Antisemitism* (Los Angeles: University of California Press, 1990). I have discussed the first of these in "The Evolution of Antisemitism," Transition 54 (1992).

people. These are character vices, in the strong sense of that word, not simply character flaws. An especially shy person may be said to have a character flaw, as may one who often becomes rambunctious at parties. A person exhibits a character flaw in being perennially late, as does the person who is too easily hurt. By contrast, a character vice is defined by inappropriate delight in and preoccupation with an activity that is pursued to such an extent that it stunts one's moral sensibilities. Most people have a regard for money, for example, but Jews as a people have been said to attach an untoward importance to the acquisition of money, thereby stunting their moral sensibilities. The propriety of the expression "irredeemably evil" is a way of saying that Jews have been thought to have this vice by their very nature, irrevocably. A poor Jew has this vice of character no less than a rich Jew, according to the stereotype.

As with Slavery and the notion of moral simpleton, a parallel question can be raised: Is the idea of the Jew as irredeemably evil compatible with the sexual exploitation of Jewish women by Nazis? Not surprisingly, I say that it is. Strictly speaking, of course, the Nazis prohibited sexual relations between Jews and "pure" Germans. The concentration camps nevertheless allowed sexual relations of any nature with Jews, and Nazis were undeterred in practicing the basest form of sexual exploitation. There is no incompatibility between ideology and practice in sexually exploiting that which is vile, as a reminder of the vileness.

I want to point out that the conception of the Jew as irredeemably evil and that of the black as a moral simpleton are fundamentally different. In fact, they probably make for an incoherent pair. Moral simpletons might do what is wrong often enough. It might even be characteristic of moral simpletons that they are lazy. But the very idea of moral simpletons' excelling at being evil is untenable. Likewise for the idea of an irredeemably evil people's being moral simpletons. Simpleminded people are thought to lack the wherewithal for full-blown evil. The two conceptions that we are dealing with are not such that one is in some sense an extension of the other. This fact, alone, suggests that extreme forms of evil, such as American Slavery and the Holocaust, ought to turn out be very different institutions. Indeed, while a society might very well have some use for moral simpletons, it is not at all clear what use a society could have for the irredeemably evil. The main difference between the Holocaust and American Slavery reflects just this fact: extermination versus the utter dependence of slavery, respectively.

Once more, the temptation to conclude that the former was obviously more evil than the latter, because death is the ultimate form of evil, should be resisted. How one survives makes all the difference in the world. As a matter of conceptual truth, it is simply false that surviving is always rationally preferable to death. However, this is to get ahead of ourselves. I want now to look directly at the institutions of the Holocaust and American Slavery.

14. *The Institutions*

It goes without saying that both American Slavery and the Holocaust were coercive institutions. Just so, they were coercive in profoundly different ways. The primary aim of the former institution was cooperative subordination, which often took exceedingly brutal forms in order to assure compliance with various norms and imperatives. The latter was purely coercive in its aim; achieving cooperation was utterly inconsequential to the primary enterprise. While the idea of cooperative subordination might seem to be incompatible with the deep cruelty of slavery, I hope to show that there is far more compatibility, and in fact far more explanatory power in this regard, than might be supposed. My position, though, is that the cruelty was far more mental than physical.

The pernicious institution of American Slavery wanted blacks to play certain roles in a white society and to perform certain tasks—lifelong roles and tasks, to be exact. The slave status of blacks was to be an integral part of society. Whites wanted blacks to believe that if blacks did their part, then whites would do right by them as slaves. In this regard slaveowners often took advantage of the good will of those who served them. To be sure, our concept of slavery does not hold slaveowners to be in any way accountable to bondsmen and -women. Slavery as an abstract notion, however, must not be confused with a given practice of the institution. If, as was the case in the United States, the aim is that slaves should be an integral part of society in well-defined subordinate roles, the arrangement works best if the subjects can accept such subordinate roles as their place in society. During American Slavery, blacks were more likely than not to accept their place in society if they believed that whites would do right by them when they performed their roles and tasks well. This is cooperative subordination.

Here is a more poignant way to put the point just made: American Slavery would not have succeeded had not a significant number of blacks to some extent adopted an internal point of view toward—that is, some measure of acceptance of—the very institution that oppressed them; this internalization made possible limited but nonetheless genuine and significant cooperation between slaves and slaveowners.[4] If society is reasonably stable, then it is simply not possible for a people who have a

---

[4]The idea of adopting an internal point of view is taken from H. L. A. Hart, *The Concept of Law* (Oxford: Clarendon Press, 1961). The members of society have the internal point of view with respect to the laws of society when they regard voluntarily acting in accordance with those laws as appropriate behavior on their part. Hart's position is that it is not possible for a society to be stable unless a substantial number of its members take the internal point of view toward the laws of their society (pp. 55–58). Hart's precise language is "the *internal aspect* of rules" (his emphasis).

subordinate role to be an integral part of a society without a measure of genuine cooperation on their part; and a measure of genuine cooperation on the part of subordinates is not possible unless they significantly internalize some of the norms of the society. The idea of people internalizing the norms of the very institutions that oppress them is hardly new.[5] Sexist ideals and values are to the detriment of women; yet women internalized them for centuries, and some women still do. Lest there be any misunderstanding, the idea of internalizing the norms that oppress one is compatible with having a great deal of ambivalence toward one's position; one need not be so besotted with one's subordinate place in the world that one gives no thought at all to a better life. On the contrary, such internalization may reflect a very firm grasp of the reality of one's situation, as well as a sense that this may be the best one can do for the moment. It is the unadorned truth that Slavery lasted some three hundred years—a very long time. It is simply not plausible to suppose that throughout those years every black was daily plotting the way to personal freedom, let alone the freedom of all blacks, even as we acknowledge that most blacks regarded slavery as a gross injustice and that some struggled valiantly against it. Finally, I should say that the idea that slaves internalized the norms of an oppressive institution hardly amounts to blaming them for the injustice they suffered.

I believe that the idea of cooperative subordination owing to some degree of internalization gets at the very heart of Eugene Genovese's claims that blacks made the best of slavery, and that the relationship between slaves and slaveowners was a most intricate one.[6] As the sexist place of women in societies shows,

[5]Cf. Herbert Marcuse, *An Essay on Liberation* (Boston: Beacon Press, 1969). I have discussed the internalization by women of sexist attitudes in my "Sexism and Racism: Some Conceptual Differences," *Ethics* 90 (1980).

[6]I am referring to his classic work, *Roll, Jordan, Roll: The World the Slaves Made* (New York: Basic Books, 1974).

whenever a people are a subordinate yet integral part of society—that is, of the lives of others—it is inevitable that a complex network of feelings will develop, both negative and positive, to which all parties are susceptible. The only reason that I shall mention is that whenever a subordinate people are an integral part of society, they are not as replaceable *in fact* as they are *in theory*. Often in spite of themselves, each side may become accustomed to the ways of the other. A slaveowner might prefer one slave to another, or a slave might be pleased or annoyed by the way one owner compared with another. The truth of the matter is that the comparison could invoke genuine pride on either side.

Frederick Douglass, for instance, noted the following:

> When Colonel Lloyd's slaves met the slaves of Jacob Jepson, they seldom parted without a quarrel about their master; Colonel Lloyd's slaves contending that he was the richest, and Mr. Jepson's slaves that he was the smartest, and most of a man. Colonel Lloyd's slaves would boast his ability to buy and sell Jacob Jepson. Mr. Jepson's slaves would boast his ability to whip Colonel Lloyd. . . . They seemed to think that the greatness of their masters was transferable to themselves. It was considered as being bad enough to be a slave; but to be a poor man's slave was deemed a disgrace indeed![7]

And thus, as Genovese indicated, given the complex role that slaveowners wanted slaves to play in the life of society, it was unavoidable that slaveowners came to have a vested interest in wanting to keep the subordinates happy.

I realize that some would object to the idea of positive feelings on either side of the slavery divide, especially the slave's, supposing that such feelings were incompatible with the nefariousness of slavery itself. Not so. First of all, this objection ignores the reality that comparative claims can be made in almost any con-

---

[7]*Narrative of the Life of Frederick Douglass: An American Slave Written by Himself*, ed. Benjamin Quarrles (Cambridge: Harvard University Press, 1988).

text whatsoever. In particular, there is nothing about the nature of an evil context itself that precludes the making of comparative judgments. Second, the objection fails to recognize that feelings of identification, gratitude, and dependency, not to mention deep expectations, need not develop consciously. In any case, they can develop in spite of one's best efforts to prevent them. What is more, these feelings are invariably context-dependent. In the context of evil, being able to count on at least some degree of good will is immeasurably preferable to being without assurance of any good will at all. A master who could be counted on for limited kindness in predictable ways was immeasurably preferable to one who reveled in arbitrariness and capriciousness. And it is a simple psychological truth that, when there is enormous evil going on all around one, nothing occasions gratitude like kindness that a person is not in any way obliged to offer—even a little kindness. The surprise, no doubt, is that nothing makes one more grateful for what little goodness there is than the very context of evil itself. This mode of thought has considerable explanatory power with respect to the cruelty of slavery.

The best evidence that there was, indeed, significant cooperation between slaves and slaveowners is those slave roles that were successful only if the slaveowners deeply trusted their slaves. This is next to impossible to see, of course, if one focuses on tasks that could be completed regardless of the attitude of the slave who performed the tasks, and that did not directly threaten one's well-being if not performed properly, such as picking cotton or cleaning a floor, although failure was annoying and undesirable, perhaps even costly at times. One might rightly surmise that these chores hardly involved much trust on the part of slaveowners. Genovese's point is that slaves were a far more integral part of society, thereby making trust an absolute prerequisite. Consider two roles of slaves that speak to this point—those of cook and nanny. The latter is more persuasive than the first.

Only a trusted slave would have the role of cook, precisely

because no slaveowners wanted to die of food poisoning. To be sure, a slave who poisoned her owners would certainly suffer dire consequences. But this point does not satisfactorily explain why a slave cook would not poison her slaveowner family. After all, even if the cook were executed for her deed, she would still have had the satisfaction of killing the family; nor, so it seems to me, could the slaveowners take much comfort in the knowledge that if they were poisoned by the cook, she would be punished by death. One thought that comes to mind is that not only the cook would be punished by death but probably her own family as well. But with this consideration, things get out of control very quickly. What is there to prevent the cook from thinking that she and all her family would be better off dead than alive? And how could the slaveowning family be sure that the cook did not think this? What if the slaveowning family should harm one of the cook's family members? Did the slaveowning family then have to fear for its own well-being? Suddenly, it looks as if having a slave cook requires such a delicate and precarious balance that slaveowners might just as soon not have had to worry about such matters. That, however, is not what happened.

There can be little doubt that slaveowners generally trusted their slave cooks; and this would have made no sense at all had the cooks not to some extent adopted the internal point of view toward slavery.

Consider, now, the nanny role, entrusting the children of slaveowners to the care of black women. This role simply cannot be understood from an entirely coercive point of view. No role could be more incompatible with pure coercion. One wants the person who cares for one's children to do so with concern for their well-being and, indeed, with affection for them. One wants the person to take a measure of pride in the flourishing of one's children. And there is no gainsaying that these favorable attitudes cannot be produced by coercion. It is thus wildly implausible to suppose that slaveowners did not worry about black caretakers' harming their children because they knew that blacks lived in dread fear of punishment if any harm befell white children. The nanny role required genuine cooperation on the part of the slave if ever a role of slavery did.

Needless to say, I do not for a moment mean to suggest that black women were so caught up in caring for white children that they gave no thought to the conditions of slavery. My argument requires only that the nanny could be counted on not to harm white children, because black slave women accepted the role of nanny. Of his mother and her master, Frederick Douglass wrote, "She had served my old master *faithfully* from youth to old age. She had rocked him in infancy, attended him in childhood, served him through life, and at his death wiped from his icy brow the cold death-sweat, and closed his eyes forever" (p. 76). His description of his mother's care for her master draws on deep affection and devotion.

Support for the line of thought that I have been pursuing comes from a condition alluded to earlier, namely the prevalence of sexism during the time of slavery. One might say that in the nanny role, slavery truly exploited the sexism of its day, according to which having and caring for one's own children were the defining features of a woman. Caring for the children of another was certainly the next best thing. On this rendering, the nanny role affirmed the womanhood of black women even as it made them victims. This rendering explains ambivalence toward the role, even as black women were generally accepting of it.

Although I have no desire to glorify the role of the nanny, we must not lose sight of the reality of life for women in general during the times of slavery. Given the depth of sexism, it is not as if black women could have pursued a host of more self-realizing options had slavery not existed. Even well-off white women generally lacked such options, to say nothing of poor white women. Nannies surely recognized this reality even as they recognized the gross injustice of the arrangement. Although a great good, freedom is by no means the only good in life. In particular, the absence of freedom does not mean that one is worse off in all other respects. Its absence for slaves—and this is one of Genovese's more profound points—certainly did not mean that any slave was worse off in all respects than any white. We can distinguish between freedom and the worth of freedom. Freedom need not always be worth very much. I believe that slaves were aware of this truth.[8] I suspect that Genovese's account of slavery is guided by this distinction.

Any number of slaves may have settled for slavery, albeit with great uneasiness. To insist otherwise is, I fear, to make the fundamental mistake of assessing the lives of slaves not from their vantage point but from ours. Of course, there were revolts and other more subtle forms of resistance on the part of slaves. But the continued existence of slavery makes it clear that not every slave so behaved. If every slave had refused to do the bidding of slaveowners, then slavery would have been no more. It will not do at this point to intone that many slaves might understandably have preferred even slavery to death or separation from their families when avoidable. Such an explanation is a concession

---

[8]In his searching work, *Freedom: Freedom in the Making of Western Culture* (New York: Basic Books, 1991), Orlando Patterson writes: "No slave, except the most degraded, such as prostitutes and robbers, wanted personal freedom where no nonslave found it worthwhile. That was like jumping from a slave ship into a shark-filled ocean. Only where the possibility existed for the isolated individual to fend for himself economically and culturally, could the slave begin even to think about his freedom as the absence of personal restraint and as doing as he pleased. No such social space ever existed before the rise of slavery in ancient Greece" (p. 42). My point in the text is that the logic of slavery alone does not entail that it is better to be free, period, than to be a slave. The point, however, does assume the significance of the color differential: In a white world, white slaves could make a better go of it than black slaves if only because white slaves could render invisible their past as slaves—not an option for black slaves in a white world. As we shall see in the following chapter (Section 16), this is an extremely significant point.

that not being a slave need not have been the highest priority to be expected of a slave. The point about the worth of freedom in the preceding paragraph assumes that it would be a mistake to suppose that freedom was the highest priority for every slave.

Before moving on, let me note that slavery produced the idea of an Uncle Tom, the servile black who knows his place among whites. Consider the following remarks by two slaves.[9] One said: "I hope prays to git to hebben. Wether I's white or black when I git dere, I'll be satisfied to see my Savior at my old marster worshippped and my husband preached 'bout. I wants to be in hebben wid all my white folks, just to wait on them and serve them, sorta lak I did in slavery time. Dat will be 'nough hebben for Adeline." Another slave had this to say: "But all and all, white folks, den were de really happy days for us niggers. Course we didn't habe de 'vantages dat we has now, but dere was sump'n back dere dat we ain't got now, an' dat secu'aty. Yassuh we had somebody to go to when we was in trouble. We had a Massa dat would fight fo' us an' help us an' laugh wid us an' cry wid us. We had a Mistus dat would nuss us when we was sick, an' comfort us when we hadda be punished." To be sure, not every slave thought about slavery in this way. Nor I have made any such claim. Presumably, however, had all slaves been fiercely fighting to free themselves of the chains of slavery, the very idea of an Uncle Tom would not have been the product of slavery.

Finally, in this vein, I note that slaves sometimes referred to themselves as "niggers." One sure sign that there has been some internalization by the oppressed of the values of the oppressor is that the oppressed refer to themselves by the same denigrating terms that the oppressor employs. Nothing analogous occurred during the Holocaust. Indeed, the term "nigger" is still sometimes used by blacks to refer to one another. Some have main-

---

[9]Both of the quotes that follow are taken from Genovese, *Roll, Jordan, Roll,* pp. 355 and 119–120, respectively.

tained that blacks are simply appropriating the language of the oppressor. I think not.

Suffice it to say that the use of "nigger" by blacks is in no way on a par with the change from "colored" or "Negro" to "black" as a term of self-reference. At one time a reference to being black was an insult; and a negative epithet was rendered even more negative when preceded by the adjective "black." However, the move to "black" as the self-referent for a people signaled a dramatic change for the better in the self-pride of blacks, who proposed that differences in skin tone among blacks should no more divide the light from the dark than like differences divide whites. This was also a case of appropriating the language of the oppressor; for a term with considerable currency was turned on its head in terms of connotation. The term "nigger" has no such history. Today, whether the speaker is black or white, calling someone black or identifying someone as a black dancer or black mayor or black salesperson is a neutral description. Not so with "nigger." It can still have thunderous derogatory connotations, whether the user is black or white.

I should like at this juncture to look at our discussion of American Slavery in light of the claim in the preceding section that the characterization of slaves as moral simpletons fits the practices of slavery.

At the outset, note that I have entirely avoided characterizing the practices of American Slavery as paternalistic.[10] The reason is not that I wish to deny that there were any paternalistic sentiments among slaveowners. Rather, I have avoided it because the issue of paternalism gets in the way. Believing that a group should occupy a subordinate role in society does not entail, and

---

[10]For an important discussion of the issue of paternalism and slavery, see Bill Lawson and Howard McGary, *Between Freedom and Slavery: Philosophy and American Slavery* (Bloomington: Indiana University Press, 1992), McGary's chapter "Paternalism and Slavery." I am indebted to McGary for helping me to realize that my argument does not require that Slavery be seen as paternalistic.

is quite distinct from, believing that one has a duty or is in any way obligated to care for the group or contribute to the betterment of its members, though the role that one assigns the group in society may very well have this effect. It is not even clear that these two beliefs have generally traveled together, since people have claimed often enough the right to the subordination of others without supposing that they had a duty to benefit their subordinates. In any event, the notion of moral simpleton is not in any way meant as a gesture toward paternalism.

Remember that European societies had appealed to class differences, pedigree, and divine right as the bases for subordinating others. In theory, at least, the United States was not having any of that. The subordination could be based only upon a natural difference, as not even a constitutional convention could undo what nature had wrought. Yet it had to be possible for the subordinated to be an integral part of society, and this assumed not only the possibility of bonding between slave and slaveowner but also the slave's capability of acting for and being guided by reasons. I believe that the notion of moral simpleton conveys the right mixture of sophistication and lack thereof. Paternalism adds nothing here; for slaveowners need not have thought it that it was good for blacks that they be treated as moral simpletons. The slaveowners need only have maintained that it would have been foolish to treat blacks as if they were capable of full moral and intellectual maturity.

It is time now to show how the ideas that have been developed do considerable justice to the view of slavery as a vicious institution. As I remarked earlier, I believe that the cruelty of slavery was far more mental than physical. Naturally, I do not mean to discount in any way the murders, beatings, and lynchings that blacks endured. I simply do not see that consideration of these physical harms fully captures the brutality of American Slavery.

A number of pages ago, I remarked that whites wanted blacks

to believe that if blacks did their part, then whites would freely do right by blacks as slaves: Whites would not arbitrarily and capriciously harm blacks but would provide them with adequate food and clothing and allow them some semblance of privacy. In a word, whites wanted blacks to trust them. Minimally, trust is understood to mean giving another reason, aside from self-interest, to believe that one will refrain from harming the other, though one could do so without loss. Or, trust is a matter of giving another reason to believe that one will benefit him or her though one could refrain from doing so without any loss whatsoever. Most significant, then, slaveowners had a stake in wanting to be seen by slaves as morally decent, even while they failed to acknowledge the full humanity of the slaves. I want to locate the cruelty of American Slavery in this very nexus of attitudes.

Frederick Douglass wrote:

> If any one thing in my experience, more than another, served to deepen my conviction of the infernal character of slavery, and to fill me with unutterable loathing of slaveholders, it was their base ingratitude to my poor old grandmother. She had served my old master *faithfully* from youth to old age. She had rocked him in infancy, attended him in childhood, served him through life, and at his death wiped from his icy brow the cold death-sweat, and closed his eyes forever. She was nevertheless left a slave—a slave for life. (p. 76, my italics)

Douglass's attack on slavery is truly revealing. It was not so much his grandmother's being in servitude that angered him as it was her master's response to her unfailing dedication to him. What was absolutely beyond Douglass's comprehension was not that her master (Douglass's former master) should have kept her a slave, but that he was not moved by her devotion, at least not enough to set her free—the master's base ingratitude. To Douglass's mind, it was this, more than anything else, that exemplified the cruelty of slavery. Let me explain.

We reveal our humanity in a variety of ways. Apropos the discussion at hand, one of the most dramatic, yet simple, ways we do so is by unequivocally meeting the complex conditions of trust and gratitude called for by social interaction. That is to say, rich trusting relationships by their very nature presuppose both moral and intellectual maturation, and acts of good will call for gratitude. Morally speaking, slaveowners simply could not have everything their way. They could not insist they were morally decent persons and demand on rich trusting relationships between themselves and slaves, all the while denying the very humanity that such relationships presuppose. Slave owners could not, morally, delight in the good will of slaves, yet show them no gratitude. This is profound moral incongruity, as I shall say; and is tantamount to toying in a most vicious way with the moral sentiments of a people. I suggest that herein lies the very depth of slavery's cruelty. It is this incongruity—*not whippings and lynchings*—to which Douglass calls attention.

A parallel would be an apprentice of five years who is told by his mentor that he is the most gifted student the teacher has seen in her sixty years of receiving students but that she will not recommend him for any job, and the fact is that without the mentor's recommendation the student's years in training are simply for naught. This situation would be cruel; and if the student has the same experience time and time again, with a different mentor in each case, there can be no doubt that this profound moral incongruity will take an enormous psychological toll on him. Now, suppose each mentor has been somewhat physically abusive as well, the student's back being covered with scars from lashings. This, obviously, would be yet another dimension of the wrong that the student has suffered. Still, I do not think that there can be any doubt where the weight of the wrong lies: in the extraordinary moral incongruity of telling the student that he is the best but that there will be no job recommendation.

The cruelty of slavery is to be understood in a like manner, both horizontally (within the same generation) and vertically (from one generation to the next). Slaves were expected to show deference to every white person, to be mindful of the concerns and needs of white people in a way that only another human being capable of intellectual and moral maturation could do, yet their full humanity was never acknowledged. It was not acknowledged even by those who had grown up with black children as playmates, or who owed their own flourishing to having been rocked in the bosom of a slave. While I should not want to trivialize the scars that the backs of slaves bore, I am nonetheless prepared to say that it is the profound moral incongruity in their day-to-day lived experiences that deepened the wounds of those physical scars. The physical scars were evidence of the profound moral incongruity of the day-to-day lived experiences of slaves.

I said at the outset that this work would not be one of invidious comparisons between the Holocaust and American Slavery. I am not making an exception here in what follows. On the contrary, I should hope it become clear how instructive a non-invidious comparison between the two can be.

There can be no doubt that the Holocaust was a purely coercive institution. The Jews were not expected to cooperate in their own deaths. Nor can the case of the *Judenrate*, the Jewish leaders' attempt to save the many by sacrificing the few, be seen as cooperation between Nazis and Jews—certainly not anything analogous to the cooperation for which American Slavery aimed. For whatever one might say of the interaction between the *Judenrate* and the Nazis, it is unmistakably clear that the aim was not to make Jews of any kind an integral part of Nazi Germany, but ultimately to exterminate them. Nor did the members of the *Judenrate* expect to be integrated into Nazi society, although some certainly had hopes of escaping the final fate that awaited them. This difference shows immediately that what we might call the continuum theory, inspired by Richard L. Rubenstein,[11] must be mistaken.

According to that theory, American Slavery occupies one place on the continuum of evil and the Holocaust is on the very same continuum, further along in the direction of evil. This entails that the latter was worse than the former. Rubenstein writes: "Slavery in North America was thus an imperfectly rationalized institution of nearly total domination under conditions of a *shortage of productive labor*. The death camp was a fully rationalized institution of total domination under conditions of a *population surplus*" (p. 41, emphasis in original). The death camps, by his account, can be rightly construed as a more fully developed form of the slavery that occurred in the United States. By his lights, American Slavery did not take the practice of domination to the high level achieved by the Holocaust. This line of reasoning fails to consider the social integration of the subordinated blacks that American Slavery aimed to achieve, with all that implied in terms of subordinated blacks' internalizing to some extent the values of the very society that was oppressing them. Thus understood, American Slavery was not about achieving total domination in the first place. If one loses sight of this, any form of slavery that one may describe will not be the slavery that occurred in the United States. As for the slavery that took place in the concentration camps, it had a different set of aims entirely. Not for a moment was there hope on the part of Nazis that Jews would internalize Nazi ideals. What is more, the labor was achieved entirely by coercion. Although we can correctly use the word "slavery" in both instances, the two were such vastly different kinds of slavery that it would be a mistake to call one a development or extension of the other. Rubenstein was misled by his focus upon domination; as our discussion of slavery

---

[11]*The Cunning of History* (New York: Harper and Row, 1975), ch. 3.

shows, the phenomenon of domination does not even approach the complexity of American Slavery. In particular, it ignores completely the profound moral incongruity of the day-to-day lived experiences of the slave. This is not a mere quibble, for the truth of the matter is that the Holocaust and American Slavery actually had logically incompatible aims. The incompatibility will become more evident as we proceed.

Most clearly, the success of the Holocaust, in contrast to that of American Slavery, did not require that Jews in any way internalize the ideology of the Holocaust as it pertained to them. Even if some Jews believed that the Holocaust was in some mysterious way the work of the Almighty, the success of the Nazi pogroms certainly did not require that belief. If the aim is extermination of a people, their beliefs are utterly irrelevant, except perhaps in a very temporal and instrumental way. Thus, the transport of Jews to their deaths was somewhat facilitated if they believed that they were going on holiday. Or, again, the moving of persons towards their deaths was made easier if, upon leaving the trains that transported them to the death camps, some Jews ran for what they wrongly believed to be Red Cross trucks.

No morally decent person reading about the Holocaust can fail to be struck by the brutality, against not only adults but infants as well. It is instructive to note that as American Slavery conceived of blacks, it did make a sharp conceptual distinction between black infants and white infants except by reference to what they would be in the future. It is no wonder that play between blacks and whites into early childhood was often permitted. If nothing of value was gained by it, certainly nothing was lost, either. There can be no greater sign of the extent to which a people is loathed than that infants and children are made to suffer the same brutal fate as the adults. This alone would suggest that the characterization of Jews as irredeemably evil accords well with Nazi practices.

Now, given the assumption that a people is irredeemably evil, complete and utter moral disentitlement of them is the only appropriate moral response. For by that assumption, it follows that there is no set of acts one could perform that would improve their moral character or make some measure of moral rehabilitation possible; nor would there be any appropriate role for them to play in one's society. One would not want them to cook for one, much less care for one's children. Instead, one would want them entirely removed from one's moral community. And if this could not be achieved by relocating them, their extermination would seem to be the only natural course of action. There would be no need to proceed mercifully, for how can the irredeemably evil be a suitable object of mercy? Brutal treatment is the only approach to a people that is consistent with the assumption that they are irredeemably evil.

It is my contention that we cannot make sense of the characterization of the Jews as irredeemably evil without the story of Satan, who was said to be the father of the Jews. As that story goes, the fall from grace of Satan the devil, who had been the angel Lucifer, is permanent. As an explanation for the permanence of that state, I suggest that any willful rejection of whatever is self-evidently and manifestly good is transforming: It transforms one from an evil person to an irredeemably evil person, as any such act expurgates or irrevocably subordinates to evil any fiber of good that might exist in one. In the Christian narrative, the Jews' rejection of Christ is the human equivalent of the devil's rejection of the Almighty; hence, the attribution that the devil is their father. Thus, if one of them is irredeemably evil, so is the other; and if the very idea of showing the devil mercy is conceptually wrong-headed, then by parity of reasoning so it must be in the case of the Jews. The Holocaust embodies the idea that evil is an inheritable character trait, for which there can be no moral, spiritual, or social remedy, and it identifies that character trait with a specific group of people, namely the Jews. It is certainly arguable that the inspiration for this comes from the Christian narrative itself.

The characterization of the Jew in Nazi ideology as irredeemably evil is more compatible with the relentless brutality that the Nazis visited upon the Jews during the Holocaust than is any other characterization one might put forward. It is the characterization that best fits the treatment of Jewish infants and children, which was as brutal as the treatment of adults. If a being is irredeemably evil, there is nothing to be said for showing mercy to it regardless of its stage of character development. One would be mistaken in showing mercy toward an irredeemably evil being whose evil character had not yet formed. Nor would one want the irredeemably evil to have the social role of a nanny or an Uncle Tom in Slavery. One would not want there to be even the pretense of affirming the irredeemably evil.

Here, then, lies the uniqueness of the Holocaust from the standpoint of the ideals of the Enlightenment. Those ideals have conceptual space for the possibility that there might be evil individuals or that an entire race of people might turn out to be intellectually inferior. But the view that an entire group of otherwise rational creatures could be inherently evil represents a profound rupture in those ideals. Nazi Germany created a moral reality where none, according to the Enlightenment, ought to have existed.

We are now in a position to make a most instructive comparison between the Holocaust and American Slavery. Embracing the ideology that a people are irredeemably evil is baldly incompatible with adopting any norms of good will toward them, whereas embracing the belief that a people are moral simpletons is, without strain, most compatible with acts of good will. Of course, any ideology can be embraced to varying degrees. The point, however, is this: When the belief that a people are irredeemably evil is embraced in full strength, it precludes believers from being part of any nonpunitive institutionalized social arrangements (any set of social practices), of whatever scale, with the people deemed to be irredeemably evil; by contrast, those who embrace in full strength the ideology that a people are moral simpletons can readily be a part of any social practices with the people so characterized.

The reason? Nonpunitive social practices are supposed to be affirming—though not necessarily to the same extent, at the same time, or in the same way—for all who participate in them; and affirmation presupposes that on some account or in some context, a person is entitled to or deserving of an expression of good will—be it no more than praise or an expression of satisfaction for a job well done, even though the person was forced to do it. American Slavery was intended as a nonpunitive social arrangement, albeit a warped one, between blacks and whites. The Holocaust was not intended as any such arrangement between Jews and Nazis. Thus, one could not have been an extension of the other, as they in fact had logically incompatible aims.

Lest there be any misunderstanding, my claim is that Slavery was intended as a nonpunitive social arrangement. I want to make two points in this regard. First, the harm that Slavery did to blacks is quite compatible with what I have claimed; there are numerous forms of interaction that are exceedingly harmful to at least one of the participants although the interaction is not a punitive one. Child sexual abuse comes to mind. Second, although it is unquestionably wrong to believe that some people deserve to be slaves, institutions that embody the view that some people deserve to be slaves are not, in so doing, punitive institutions. Our understanding of the wrong of American Slavery is not enhanced by supposing that it was by nature an institution that systematically punished black people unjustly.

The difference between the Holocaust and American Slavery regarding norms of good will sheds light on yet another difference. Regardless of the brutality of the Holocaust, there were times when Jews in the death camps were grateful for this or that behavior of a Nazi. How was it possible for Jews to feel any gratitude towards Nazis? Similarly, many have found preposterous the suggestion by Genovese that some slaves in the United States were loyal to their masters, to say nothing of the idea that the owners expected it. The formal answer is this. Under nonpunitive social arrangements, there is a possibility not only of gratitude between peoples but also of loyalty between members who participate in the arrangement. If the social arrangements between peoples are punitive, on the other hand, only gratitude is possible. Loyalty requires belief that one can play a role in another's life, whereas gratitude requires only the belief that another has benefited one. Although the benefit must be intended, it need not be owing to a longstanding desire to see the beneficiary well off. What is more, in bestowing the benefit, the person may be acting completely out of character, as was the case with Dr. Ernst B., the Nazi medical doctor in Auschwitz 22 who was introduced earlier.[12] How did a Nazi doctor manage to earn the gratitude of Holocaust survivors? In the words of one survivor:

> [Dr. B.'s] very first visit to the lab of Block 10 . . . was an extraordinary surprise for us. He came into the lab without force unlike the other SS, without a dog (Weber always came with a dog), locked the doors behind him [so that his behavior could not be observed by other SS], said "Good day" and introduced himself, . . . offering his hand to my colleagues and me. . . . We were . . . long unused to anyone from among the camp authorities treating us as people equal to himself.[13]

As noted earlier, Dr. B. did not participate in the selections that sent Jews to their deaths, not on the grounds that selections were wrong but that he lacked the wherewithal to do so. On the negative side, it should be mentioned that never once in his interview with Robert Lifton did Dr. B. concede that the attempt to exterminate the Jews was a mistake.

---

[12]For the account of Dr. Ernst B., see Robert Lifton, *Nazi Doctors* (New York: Basic Books, 1986).

[13]Quoted from Lifton, p. 303.

What I want to draw attention to is how grateful prisoners were for even the gestures of humanity that they received from Ernst B. In a context where everything was a reminder that Jews were more expendable than cattle, a handshake and a greeting took on astonishingly humanity-affirming qualities. Limited though they were, such gestures were nonetheless relief from the inhumane environment of Auschwitz, and for that alone the Jews were immensely grateful. When Ernst B. in fact saved the life of a Jew—and he did not do so in all cases—then a trickle of relief became a veritable oasis.

There were sporadic acts of beneficence in the death camps; even more rare were instances of a beneficence of a more systematic sort by the likes of Ernst B. In the moral abyss of Auschwitz, it was not possible for a Jew to play anything remotely resembling an affirming role in the life of a Nazi. The Jews did not play that role in Ernst B.'s life, nor did he want them to. More to the point, nothing analogous to the role of the slave Uncle Tom could have existed during the Holocaust, even bearing in mind that the Uncle Tom referred to an institutional ideal of the good black that not everyone embraced. The only good Jew, from the standpoint of the institution of the Holocaust, was a dead Jew.

The story of Dr. Ernst B. and the contrast between an institution of evil that is incompatible with norms of good will and an institution that is not should enable us to see how it was possible for there to be loyalty between slaves and slaveowners. Frederick Douglass's mother was clearly loyal to her master even in Douglass's eyes. It is true that slaves were subordinate to slaveowners, but that subordination was compatible with there being significant roles for the former to play in the lives of the latter. Taking oppression as a given, it is better to have at least some significance in the lives of those who oppress one. If a black came to cherish having that significance, which as the quote from the slave Adeline makes clear was surely possible, then that black had already made a start down the road of loyalty.

This account is consistent with the claim that the evil of slavery lay in the profound moral incongruity in the day-to-day lives of slaves. Talk of loyalty among animals notwithstanding, loyalty at its richest is ineluctably a human psychological attitude precisely because it entails an identification with the aims of another. Nothing could be more incongruous than to revel in the loyalty of another but deny the full moral maturity of the other.

I want to conclude this chapter with some comments on the way in which I have characterized the difference between the Holocaust and American Slavery, specifically, about what might appear to be a failure to avoid any invidious comparison between them. It might be asked whether the Holocaust did not give rise to a profound moral incongruity in the day-to-day lived experiences of the Jews, as Slavery did in the case of blacks. In my view the Holocaust preyed upon a single emotion, namely fear. It denied that Jews had any claim whatsoever to good will; any good will shown to a Jew in the camps was simply a matter of whim. There were no arrangements, no practices, and no set of activities that were in any way contrary to the view that the Jews had no claim against Nazi society. It is common enough for a person to be deserving of something without having a right to it. A person can be clearly deserving of the first-place prize in a contest but have no right to it because it was awarded to someone else by a corrupt set of judges. The Nazis not only denied that the Jews had any rights under the Nazi state to being treated with good will, but even denied that they were a fit object of any measure of good will. In this case, talk of moral incongruity in the day-to-day lived experiences of the Jews completely misses the mark, at least as I have used the notion in connection with American Slavery. The brutality of the Holocaust lies in its relentless denial that Jews were deserving of any good will; there were no incongruities of social practice at all.

The Holocaust was morally eviscerating: It maintained that human beings were undeserving of any form of good will, and so, a fortiori, any form of justice. The Holocaust did not deny the humanity of the Jew, as many are inclined to say. Rather, it insisted that their humanity had a peculiarity to it that rendered them beyond the reach of all of morality. Had Jews been considered nonhuman creatures, they could not also have been considered irredeemably evil. To be sure, Jews were called vermin. But I take it to be obvious that "vermin" was a metaphor for that which was exceedingly filthy, morally speaking.

Which is preferable, being a victim of morally incongruous institutions or being a victim of morally eviscerating institutions? No doubt by some demented yardstick an answer is possible. But so too might it be possible to answer the question, Who has suffered more: the person who has lost both legs or the person who has lost both arms?

A reasonable person could read the preceding two paragraphs—nay, this entire chapter—with both approval and relief, yet feel dissatisfied. Allowing that moral incongruity and moral evisceration must each be taken on its own terms, there is yet this difference: Ultimately, the Holocaust intended the wrongful death of the Jews, whereas American Slavery, for all its nefariousness, did not intend the wrongful death of black people. I take up this matter in the following chapter.[14]

[14] In writing this chapter, I wish to express my indebtedness to Bill Lawson, who has argued that slavery left blacks in a state of political limbo. See his essays "Citizenship and Slavery" and "Moral Discourse and Slavery" in Bill Lawson and Howard McGary, *Between Slavery and Freedom: Philosophy and American Slavery* (Indianapolis: Indiana University Press, 1992). I accept the substance of Lawson's views.

Murderous Extermination and Natal Alienation

15. Doing Justice to the Difference

Death has no equal in foreclosing options. Whatever may follow this life on earth, human beings know not of it. Death is so dreaded that even in the depths of moral squalor around them, it is rare for people to take their own lives; and when they do, we are often inclined to think that they have performed an act of courage. Slaves did not rush to take their lives during either American Slavery or the Middle Passage voyage from Africa that preceded it. Jews during the Holocaust did not rush to take their lives, though conditions of the concentration camps were unsuitable even for animals. As these remarks are expanded upon, some points made earlier will be repeated to obtain juxtaposition helpful to the discussion.

Undeniably, the killing of six million Jews accounts in part for the moral horror of the Holocaust—though, as I noted in the Introduction, the horror is due not only to the murderous deaths as such but, even more repugnant, to the near-extermination of a people. Murder is an intentional, inexcusable killing, and no account of the Holocaust can lose sight of that. Even unintentional killings can reveal bone-chilling indifference, as when a person drives recklessly in a display of bravado; but indifference to the death of another as the consequence of one's actions (when one is not intending to kill in the first place) is not as fulsome as intending or desiring that person's death. By definition, the murder of another person cannot be unintentional, much less can the murder of six million people. With death being what it is, murder being what is, and the extermination of a people being what it is—to say nothing of the maniacal cruelty that was inflicted along the way—how can anyone fail to conclude that the Holocaust represents an ultimate form of evil? The Holocaust has a special place in Jewish history itself. The Inquisition, which resulted in the murder of many, many Jews, is not thought to have been the equal of the Holocaust. It should not occur to anyone, however, that the significance that the Holocaust has in Jewish thought is meant to diminish the suffering that Jews have otherwise endured.

American Slavery was not about the mass murder of a people with extermination as its ultimate aim; dead people do not make good slaves. No story will change that. All the same, this does not mean that the loss of the lives of millions of black people counts for nothing. It does mean, though, that we do well to refrain from calling that loss something that it is not. Whether or not the loss of slaves during the Middle Passage exceeded the number of deaths among Jews during the Holocaust, that loss was not owing to an attempt to exterminate blacks.

It is my belief that the preoccupation with the death toll of evil institutions—as if death were the only dimension of evil, and so the number of deaths the only criterion of the magnitude of evil—has prevented those who would do justice to the evil of Slavery from doing just that. Evil is not impoverished. To make clear that the evil of the Holocaust is not simply a function of the number of Jews who lost their lives, I have cited three combined factors: murder, the attempt to exterminate, and the cruelty that was inflicted along the way. Take away the reality that the Holocaust brought the Jewish people to the brink of extermination, and the magnitude of its evil would change, just as the significance of the wrong owing to lives lost during the slave trade would change dramatically had that loss brought blacks to the brink of extermination. For extermination marks not just an increase in the ordinality of the number of people killed, but qualitatively changes for the worse the character of the harm done by those killings. If more than numbers matter in characterizing the evil of the Holocaust, more than numbers might matter in characterizing other evil institutions as well.

This brings me to the concept of natal alienation. There is natal alienation in the lives of an ethnic group when the social practices of the society into which they are born forcibly prevent most of them from fully participating in, and thus having a secure knowledge of, their historical-cultural traditions.[1] It must also be true that the group's members are not given full membership in the society; hence, their very lived experiences serve as reminders that they have lost out on two accounts, as they have neither equality nor their historical-cultural traditions. This refinement is meant to allow for the theoretical possibility that a people who have been prevented from participating in their own historical-cultural traditions may yet flourish as equals in a society. Natal alienation is not an all-or-nothing matter, since neither are historical-cultural traditions. What is more, it can be arrested or entirely reversed. For instance, a people who has been natally alienated either partially or completely could come upon its kind elsewhere in the world where the traditions of the group are well in place. Finally, let me say, for the sake of completeness, that it can be a matter of considerable debate whether a people has been natally alienated, for not all historical-cultural

[1] I borrow the idea of natal alienation from Orlando Patterson, *Slavery and Social Death* (Cambridge: Harvard University Press, 1982). I should like to think that my usage of the term is faithful to his intentions.

traditions are equally definitive of a people. The matter of degree of course raises the question of which traditions must survive in order for it to be true that a people has not been natally alienated.

A factor most relevant to whether the harm of natal alienation occurs and the extent to which it does is time: the longer the members of an ethnic group are exposed to oppressive institutions that are natally alienating, the more likely it is that they will become natally alienated. The reason is that substantial natal alienation of an ethnic group can take place over several generations. The first generation of an ethnic group subjected to natally alienating institutions will have firsthand knowledge of their historical-cultural traditions, since prior to the subjugation this generation will have fully (that is, actively and directly) participated in the historical-cultural traditions of its people—and, let us assume, in an environment that affirms its doing so. Accordingly, individuals belonging to this generation will have a vivid sense of who they are historically and culturally that can come only in the wake of direct participation in one's historical-cultural traditions. For these reasons, the lives of those belonging to the first generation will bear a full imprimatur, let us say, of their historical-cultural traditions; and the significance of this imprimatur in their lives cannot be eradicated by being subjugated to natally alienating institutions, although the individuals are no longer able to particulate fully in their historical-cultural traditions. By contrast, the lives of those in the very next generation, the first born into natally alienating institutions will not—indeed, cannot—have a full imprimatur of the cultural-historical traditions that belong to their people. At best, they will have firsthand reports from those with a full imprimatur. By the fourth and fifth generations, however, it is clear that not only will no one among the subjugated people be fully participating in the historical-cultural traditions of their people, but worse yet there will be few, if any, firsthand reports from those who did so. By the seventh generation, of course, there will be no surviving members bearing a full imprimatur of their historical-cultural traditions.

After seven generations of having been subjugated to very natally alienating institutions, an ethnic group's historical-cultural traditions can no longer be seriously defined in terms of the historical-cultural traditions that were theirs prior to the oppression. Or, at any rate, there will be two different historical-cultural traditions, even if the latter is an offshoot of the former. For historical-cultural traditions survive only insofar as individuals can fully participate in the practices that define them; and precisely what natally alienating institutions do is make such participation impossible by ensuring that the practices definitive of the historical-cultural traditions simply do not survive.

Lest there be any misunderstanding, I do not hold that it takes seven generations for natal alienation to occur. In particularly unjust circumstances, natal alienation could occur in considerably less time; in less unjust circumstances, it could take longer to occur. I am writing with American Slavery in mind. With that institution being what is was, it is undeniable, I assume, that natal alienation had set in by the seventh generation of slaves, though no doubt it had set in sooner.

Now, with a kind of rhetorical flourish, someone might want to say that death is the ultimate form of natal alienation. I should like to resist this rhetorical move. I prefer to hold, instead, that neither a dead person nor an exterminated people can be natally alienated. Natal alienation, I shall insist, requires a living subject.

Was the Holocaust natally alienating? The question must be properly delimited. There were culturally rich Jewish communities in Poland, for example. Those social communities were virtually decimated. The language of Yiddish, for instance, is on the verge of extinction. Hitler's aim, however, was not to murder Jews in this or that social community, but Jews of whatever persuasion. The question must be, then, whether the Holocaust was natally alienating of Jews as such, without regard to any specific community of Jews. Thus understood, the answer is that the Holocaust was not. It might be thought that I am committed to saying that it was not, given the statements in the preceding paragraph that natal alienation requires a living object and that it requires time. One could choose to stand on the formality of the account. Thus, if one takes the Holocaust to have begun with Kristallnacht in 1938 and to have ended with the end of World War II, one could insist that the Holocaust, covering less than a decade, did not last long enough to render Jews natally alienated. And these dates seem reasonable enough, since the Holocaust represents an especially virulent period of anti-Semitism, with other periods of anti-Semitism, sometimes quite virulent ones, existing on either side of the Holocaust. But formal moves are almost never satisfying when it comes to settling substantive issues. Since the Holocaust did not succeed in the aim of exterminating the Jews, to insist that it could not have been natally alienating because it did not last long enough is to settle far too substantive an issue by a merely formal point. The Holocaust was not natally alienating, though, because the central tenets of Judaism—the defining traditions of Judaism endured in spite of Hitler's every intention to the contrary. No Jew who survived the Holocaust was at a loss as to how to recover the traditions of Judaism.

Recovering the traditions of Judaism was not a concern that plagued Jews who settled in what became the nation of Israel or in the United States or anywhere else. No one wondered what counted as a Bar Mitzvah or Bat Mitzvah or how to perform them. No one wondered what rituals to perform for Pesach, or what the Four Questions of Pesach were. After the Holocaust the Jewish tradition, in all of its richness, was left very much intact. If the Holocaust emptied those traditions of any meaning, it is certainly not because it left Jews at a loss to identify those traditions belonging to Judaism.

Does this mean, then, that the Holocaust was not the nefarious institution that we have taken it to be? Certainly not. It simply means what we already know, namely that the Holocaust was not evil in every respect. Nor was Slavery.

It can come as no surprise that I shall maintain that American Slavery succeeded in natally alienating blacks.

By the 1650s Slavery was well established in the United States. By 1750 there were more slaves in the United States who had been born there than who had been forcibly brought there. And by 1860 virtually all slaves in the United States had been born there, since the slave trade ended around 1808. Taking a generation to be twenty years, Slavery in the United States was in full force for at least ten generations.

For awhile, at least, the number of slaves with firsthand memories of their past, whose lives thus bore the full imprimatur of their African historical-cultural traditions, exceeded the number of slaves who had been born into Slavery. The very first slaves were not born into Slavery being called "nigger," nor in Africa was the darkness of the color of their skin the decisive mark of their inferiority. They knew firsthand what Slavery had deprived them of. That skin color came to be the decisive mark of inferiority in Slavery is very important here, for it enables us to put into perspective the claim that Africans enslaved one another.

Whatever slavery in Africa might have been like, it had to have been qualitatively different from American Slavery, if only because of skin color. We can see this simply in terms of escaping. African slavery must have been more clearly defined by the control that the master asserted over the slaves than by the attitudes of society at large. If a slave in Africa could escape from that control, he would then find anonymity as one black among many. To be sure, there would be the risk of discovery, but it was not skin color that would call attention to a slave in Africa. His skin color would no more have been the focus of concern than the fact that he had two feet. Not so in America, where color meant everything. Although there were some free Negroes, they had at best a very local freedom, meaning that they could count on being even minimally treated as free only in the community that knew them to be free. It was not the freedom to go where they liked. In the United States, a slave who showed up in an unfamiliar place claiming to be free would only be thought a runaway. If this was not obvious to Africans when they first arrived, they found out soon enough the decisive significance of their skin color in America.

In the beginning, nearly all slaves had a past that they had lived in Africa. The generations after them were slaves born in the United States. To be sure, some second-, third-, and possibly even fourth-generation slaves born in America had secondhand accounts of firsthand imprimaturs of life in Africa. But to have a secondhand account of freedom, no matter how vividly told, is not even to come close to experiencing freedom itself—certainly not for those in the context of American Slavery. This is not to deny the richness of narratives. The point, rather, is that the blacks born into Slavery were bereft of any experiences that could anchor the narratives of Africa. Nor could they look across from their social reality and fix their gaze upon the freedom of Africa, in the way that a person born into poverty can see, if only from afar, how the well-off live. Not only that, the very first generation of American-born slaves were slaves from birth and knew their parents only as slaves, whatever their parents might have been in Africa. By the fifth generation, it was not only that there were more American-born slaves than African-born, but the percentage of their parents who were American-born was also considerably higher than the percentage born in Africa.

Given the character of Slavery, it is thus most unlikely that the historical-cultural traditions of Africa would come to have a secure foothold among slaves in the United States. Time and the conditions of Slavery itself were a barrier that allowed very little of substance to pass through.

It might be said in response that a rich oral tradition (story telling) and a rich tradition of rhythm in both dance and song was transplanted from Africa to America via Slavery. Can anyone deny this? The influence of blacks in American popular music and dance is both unmistakable and indelible. There is no mistaking the African imprint upon the cadence of Jesse Jackson or Martin Luther King, Jr. This influence of Africa cannot be denied without flying in the facing of reality. But it is not rich enough to have secured the self-identity of a people through historical-cultural traditions.

An essential requirement in this regard is a narrative (most often a set of narratives) that defines values and positive goals and fixes points of historical significance and ennobling rituals that cannot be readily appropriated. We may say that the narratives of a people define their conception of the good, while providing both significant historical reference points that anchor various values and ennobling rituals. Narratives can also have a shameful aspect to them; and they are not necessarily fixed. Most interesting, narratives need not be true as such but are a kind of folklore of value that serves as a point of reference. In any case, they connect the past with the future, even the ones that have shameful aspects to them. It goes without saying that narratives may benefit some at the expense of others and may in fact be harmful to those who embrace them. Some would say that the narrative of the traditional male has disfavored women with a vengeance, and has perhaps done more than a little damage to the men who aspire to live up to it as well. And this narrative has been, and in many instances continues to be, a part of the traditions of some of the most powerful institutions in society, including religious and academic sectors. What is more, the narrative is often rife with distortions.[2]

My claim, then, is that unless there are narratives from Africa that were operative in the ideals and values that slaves forged, the combination of the oral and the rhythmic traditions is not sufficient to yield African historical-cultural moorings for blacks in America. For example, to know that an object came from one's great-grandparents and that it had extraordinary value to them is clearly to know the source of its family significance. It is not, however, the same as knowing the nature of that significance. Hence, the nature of its significance can hardly play a role in shaping one's ideals and values. Similarly, to know the historical source of a pattern of behavior is not thereby to know the pattern's significance; nor is it to know the narrative that accompanied that pattern of behavior. Accordingly, valuing a pattern of behavior that is tied to one's ancestors, as important and as understandable as that can be, since that may be all that is left, is not by itself tantamount to having one's life informed by the narrative that was attached to that behavior. While patterns of behavior are most often constitutive of narratives, behavioral patterns, regardless of the significance attached to them, do not by themselves make a narrative nor can they stand in for one.

[2]Given their portrayal in American culture, homosexual cowboys seem to be fictitious creatures. But they were not. See John D'Emilio, *Intimate Matters: A History of Sexuality in America* (New York: Harper and Row, 1988). I am very grateful to Jennifer Parkhurst for bringing this work to my attention. It also contains a fascinating account of levels of affection displayed, in correspondence and physically, between men at Harvard in the 1800s—displays that in our time would be taken as decisive evidence of a man's homosexuality but that occasioned no such thought then. Before homosexuality was declared a disease of the mind, acts of homosexuality were merely acts that society frowned upon in the way that society now frowns upon theft. Acts of thievery do not generally invite the thought that a person is suffering from some mental disorder. So men in the 1800s did not need to distance themselves physically, lest it be thought by anyone that they had the "mental disease" of homosexuality.

Consider the black church. It is one of the most expressive institutions in America. The deliverance style of the preacher, the singing of the choir, and the spiritual rejoicing that often enough gives rise to the spiritual dancing called shouting are all said to have their roots in African traditions.[3] I should hardly deny this. What I am denying, though, is that present church style that is thought to be characteristically black owes anything to an African narrative. Nor need this connection exist for it to be true that had it not been for the oral and rhythmic traditions blacks might not have survived Slavery as well as they did.

Absolutely telling against the idea that black religious tradition is informed by an African narrative is the unmistakably Christian nature of the black religious tradition in the United States, for Africa is utterly irrelevant to the Christian narrative. For all of its expressive power, the Negro spiritual is unequivocally Christian in the content of its message. Blacks may have given Christian worship in their lives an unmistakable African cadence, but they have done so as Christians, which can only mean that it is they and not Christianity that underwent the greater transformation. Symbolically, there is no greater sign of acquiescing to another people, nor a more radical departure from one's own past, than the accepting of their god as one's own, whether this is done with great fanfare or in infinitesimally small steps. Accepting the god of another people may very well be the morally right thing to do. That does not change in any way the symbolic significance of doing so. Only at the price of inconsistency, then, can a person acknowledge Christianity as a powerful force in the lives of blacks, during Slavery and since,

[3]See Sterling Stuckey, *Slave Culture: Nationalist Theory and the Foundations of Black America* (New York: Oxford University Press, 1987), who is concerned to show that American black culture is basically African at its roots. Stuckey suggests that the "shout" had great meaning in African contexts (p. 88). I say more about these matters in the following chapter.

yet insist that Slavery wrought no significant natal alienation in their lives.

Without intending any indictment of Christianity itself, it must be noted how well it served the ends of Slavery. First of all, it is not an egalitarian doctrine with respect to power and material things, at times suggesting that the poor have a better chance of getting to heaven. Second, and this is related to the first, it is an otherworldly doctrine. The true self is the spiritually whole self, and that self is to have its full realization in the world to come. The deprivations that one must endure on earth are held to be nothing compared with the riches that one will enjoy in heaven. Third, Christianity insists both that charity is the greatest of all gifts and that one must not hold lack of charity against any fellow human being. One must forgive him instead. Could a religious doctrine be more suited to the conditions of Slavery without actually condoning it? It is hard to imagine how. If Christianity had not been operating, something like it would have been well worth inventing for the purposes of Slavery. A doctrine that allows for slave and master to be equals in the very same heaven but demands obedience by the former to the latter on earth is more than a little accommodating to injustice.

It is true that slaves sometimes employed Christian doctrine to stay the master's hand. But what is striking is that in general the slaves did not view their own bondage as an outright indictment of Christianity, a phenomenal embarrassment to the religion. To believe in the god of another people is one thing; to believe in the god of a people who so visibly oppress one, by appealing to the words of their god, is quite another. People in general reject even deeply cherished religious convictions in the face of continuing suffering, whereas blacks seem to have embraced Christianity with vigor. I regard the acceptance of the religious traditions of one's oppressor as the most telling sign of natal alienation possible. There could be no greater evidence of the complexity of the relationship between master and slave under American Slavery than that this acceptance could happen. The relationship simply could not have been an entirely hostile one.

16.   Ultimates in Evil: Alienation and Extermination

To produce natal alienation in a people is to render them without a narrative. This is no small harm. One does not wish to offend with too imaginative an example, but suppose that over ten generations there were no ritual circumcisions, no Bat or Bar Mitzvahs, no synagogues, and no conversions; suppose, also, that over ten generations, Jewish women had fewer and fewer children because as a result of social indoctrination their sense of worth became ever more tied to caring for the children of others rather than bearing children, and that children born of Jewish women were separated from their families at birth and raised as non-Jews. If all of these things happened over ten generations, it is not clear that anyone could say with any confidence that the Jews as an ethnic group would still exist—at least not by the criteria by which Jewishness has traditionally been determined. By the tenth generation, it would be well-nigh impossible for anyone to know who had been born of a Jewish woman. In such an instance, the Jews would have been natally alienated, although as I have told the story no one would have been killed.

This shows at once that mass murder by itself is not a necessary condition if the survival of a people as a group is to be systematically and perhaps irreversibly undermined. To be sure, no people can survive as a people given the deaths of all of its members. But one reasons fallaciously in supposing that in the absence of the deaths of all or nearly all of its members, a people can be said to survive as a people. Because skin color is often taken as decisive when it comes to determining ethnic identification, and because by that measure it is clear that people of African descent survived Slavery, it is easy for the natally alienating character of slavery, profound though it was, to go unappreciated. If it is obvious that people of African descent survived Slavery, what is anything but obvious is defining the identity of what survived. Only if one trivializes the practices that were definitive of the historical-cultural traditions of Africans prior to their enslavement can one possibly think it obvious which black identity survived, or regard the matter as inconsequential. It may be obvious that all blacks have their origins in Africa. But Africa is a large continent populated by diverse groups. So to take it for granted that many Americans came from Europe but only one people came from Africa is surely a form of cultural arrogance.

The conclusion to be drawn here is not that natal alienation is on par with extermination, but that natal alienation is, or certainly can be, an extraordinary evil that has nothing whatsoever to do with death. For those who would insist that survival is the greater good, even if the survivors are deracinated from their historical-cultural traditions, an experiment in thinking might be helpful. Suppose you belong to a group whose ennobling rituals, practices, and identity you cherish. You must choose either the extermination or the complete and irreversible alienation of that group. There are no other options. Which would it be rational to choose? The choice between extermination and mere slavery would, by comparison, be easy. Folklore even has it that there have been celebrated deliverances from slavery. In hopes of release, a rational person would certainly choose slavery. The choice between extermination and natal alienation, on the other hand, is not an easy one. Suddenly, it becomes painfully clear that there is more to life than mere existence. Between extermination and natal alienation, one chooses without hope. It is precisely that glimmer of hope that makes the choice between extermination and mere slavery a remarkably easy one. To focus on the lived experiences of American Slavery and ignore its natally alienating impact would, in the case of the Holocaust, be analogous to focusing on the number of Jews who were killed while ignoring the impact that this was intended to have upon the very existence of Jews as a people.

If the arguments of this chapter are sound, then the machinery for a certain kind of invidious comparison has been dismantled or, at any rate, seriously impaired.

The extermination of a people is determined not only by the number killed, though numbers are clearly relevant. Neither is natal alienation determined only by the number of people who are left without any historical moorings, though here, too, numbers are clearly relevant. In each case, the structure that accounts for the numbers affected is of ineliminable importance, and not merely a minor detail that can be added to round out a thought, space or time permitting. And we have seen that the structure of murderous extermination and that of natal alienation are most dissimilar; neither is an extension of the other. If each structure is, respectively, the defining feature of the Holocaust and American Slavery, then neither of these two evil institutions is an extension of the other.

I have argued that American Slavery had a feature to it, namely natal alienation, that the Holocaust did not have. From this, it does not follow that Slavery was more evil than the Holocaust. The morally eviscerating character of the Holocaust is hardly diminished by the fact that it was not natally alienating. On the contrary, for I have also argued that norms of benevolence operated in American Slavery, but not the Holocaust. And I have argued that the latter was decisively coercive against Jews, but that the former involved a measure of cooperation on the part of blacks. Yet, I have not suggested that American Slavery was either less or more evil than the Holocaust. The psychological scar of Slavery is that it was natally alienating; the psychological scar of the Holocaust is that the Nazis found a way not just to wrong innocent human beings, namely Jews, but to regard and treat them as inherently evil. These are deep, deep scars that are radically different.

To conclude this section, it is useful to distinguish between two ways of understanding the claim that X is an ultimate evil: 1. No evil can be more horrible than X; 2. All other evils are less horrible than X. The first would allow that at least one other evil, say Y, is as horrible as X. The second, by contrast, entails that Y—any Y—must be less horrible than X. I should like to suggest that the Holocaust and American Slavery are best understood as ultimate evils in the first sense, as this way of understanding precludes even the appearance of invidious comparisons. Only extremely unsavory motives could explain a person's insistence that one (and only one) of these institutions must be regarded as an ultimate evil in the second of the two senses delineated above.

17. Self-Hatred

Self-hatred is a deep dissatisfaction with aspects of oneself, stemming from a longing to be accepted by others. Self-hatred can be based upon membership in a group that is thought to have some moral or intellectual shortcoming, upon shame at having physical features that readily identify a person as belonging to such a group, or upon the person's shame at various forms of behavior that are thought to be characteristic of the group.

In any account of the experiences of blacks and Jews, it must be allowed that some self-hatred occurred in the lives of some of them, at least to some degree, for self-hatred is not an all-or-nothing matter. We naturally want to distance ourselves from unjustified negative assessments of who we are or what we do. But this is difficult to do when such assessments are a pervasive aspect of the very society in which we live, and when much of our day-to-day life is a reminder that if we were white or had a smaller nose or had straighter hair or whatever, then we would not have had this or that negative experience, or at the very least we would not have to steel ourselves for the possibility of such an encounter. It is psychologically jarring to live in a society that professes rationality and good will but that excludes one on the basis of a trait irrelevant to the enterprise at hand. When day-to-day life would be much easier if only one lacked this or that trait, it is not surprising to wish that one were without it. And if the trait truly gets in the way of the endeavor to live a meaningful life, it would be next to impossible, psychologically, not to experience a little self-hatred on account of having the characteristic in question. This much is obvious. I have broached the topic of self-hatred not to explicate it, but for the sake of completeness.

Given the account of natal alienation offered, it stands to reason that a people who are victims of natal alienation will also, to varying degrees, experience self-hatred. What does not follow from this, however, is that a people who have not experienced natal alienation will not experience self-hatred.⁴ That there has been, and continues to be, self-hatred among Jews is surely indisputable. But, as one would imagine, the self-hatred that infects the lives of a people will be very much a function of the nature of their experiences. The considerations of this chapter and others in this book suggest a difference between black self-hatred and Jewish self-hatred. The self-hatred of blacks has its basis in wanting to achieve moral and social recognition, whereas the self-hatred of Jews has its basis in wanting not to be seen as a threat to the moral and social order. Blacks suffer from an untoward kind of invisibility; Jews suffers from an untoward kind of visibility. In the prologue of his novel *Invisible Man*, Ralph Ellison with breathtaking eloquency insists that white people have difficulty seeing even the black person who bumps into them. This is not stated as the literal truth, of course. And

---

⁴I am grateful to Harold Brackman of the Simon Wiesenthal Center for raising the issue. The remarks in the text are a response to his concern.

Ellison was as aware as anyone that whites have often viciously attacked blacks who (were merely thought to have) stepped out of line. I take Ellison's point to be that only a kind of moral and social invisibility could explain that blacks have so little standing in American society, although they have played significant roles in the lives of whites, including that of child caretaker. At the very least, one would think that the whites in whose lives blacks played such a role would have accorded blacks equal moral and social visibility. Not so. Ellison's prologue brilliantly illustrates that not even those whites were moved. After all, when one is playing a significant role in the life of others, one is too much a part of their moral and social space not to "bump" into them quite frequently. This profound moral incongruity is the source of black self-hatred.

Jews have never been invisible in this way. What is more, anti-Semitism has never questioned the wherewithal of Jews to be agents; quite the contrary, the problem is, and has always been, that a morally inappropriate form of agency is systematically and unjustifiably said to be a definitive feature of being a Jew. The many forms of Jewish assimilation that are fueled by self-hatred are often meant to convey to the world that Jews are not of the questionable moral character that has been wrongly attributed to them.

Two final comments. First, the above remarks concerning the source of black self-hatred are compatible with contemporary black urban violence. This is so, at any rate, if one supposes, as I do, that such violence is quite often a desperate plea for moral and social visibility. A defense of this claim, however, would take us beyond the purview of this essay. Second, I take it to be obvious that no road to self-hatred is better than others, and that self-hatred as such is bad, regardless of the form it might take. Only the morally demented could suppose that, between black and Jewish self-hatred, one is more palatable than the other.

PART III

Surviving into the Future

After the Ashes

If American Slavery and the Holocaust were equally wicked institutions, how does one explain the radical difference in the way blacks and Jews have survived their respective evils, certainly in the United States? Of course, the fact that two institutions were on a par in terms of evil hardly entails that the victims of each should recover in the same way and at the same rate, if only because the differences between institutions can affect their victims in radically different ways. Still, the question does not lose its force. On the whole it would seem that Jews have flourished since the Holocaust, while blacks have languished since American Slavery. While this may be taken as a comparison between blacks and Jews, I have not put it forth as such. Regardless of the existence of Jews, it could still be said that blacks have languished; and even if blacks did not exist, Jews could still be said to have flourished, though perhaps the way each group has fared is brought into sharper relief by the way things have transpired for the other.

The explanation for the difference cannot be solely the virulent racism that continued beyond Slavery; for neither did anti-Semitism cease with the end of the Holocaust, but expressed itself quite virulently on American soil, even in some of its finest

educational institutions. Nor can the explanation be the economic differential between blacks and Jews, since many Jews
came to America poor. It is precisely these truths that seem to
energize the question with which I began, allowing that institutions can affect people differently.

Before getting underway, perhaps a caveat is in order. Rather
than discussing the comparative successes of blacks and Jews in
the United States, it might seem more appropriate to compare
the successes of the two groups on the very continents where
they were victims of their respective institutions. For it can be
observed that while Jews in both the United States and Canada
have flourished since the Holocaust, Jews in other countries
have not done nearly so well. This line of reasoning might continue as follows: Blacks, unlike Jews, were slaves in the United
States, and that is the fundamental difference between the two
people, which explains the differential in their successes. No
doubt there is more than enough rhetorical force to silence those
would like to continue the inquiry. But we should ask: How
does Slavery explain blacks' lack of success in the United States?
What is more, while it is certainly true that Jews were never
slaves in the United States, it hardly follows that their success in
America is explained by that fact alone. If there is some factor of
relevance to the success of Jews that Slavery denied to blacks,
that would be significant indeed. That would make discussing
the differential between blacks and Jews in the United States
worthwhile, notwithstanding the truth of the initial points with
which I began these remarks.

18.   *Jews*

How does one explain the flourishing of so many Jews, who
arrived destitute in America nearly eighty years after Slavery,
while blacks continued to languish? One explanation that must

be considered is what we may call the social invisibility thesis. Ultimately, though, I shall attach far greater weight to a different thesis.

In the early 1920s President Lawrence Lowell of Harvard University was, in effect, calling on the social invisibility thesis when he said: "Cambridge could make a Jew indistinguishable from an Anglo-Saxon; but not even Harvard could make a black man white."[1] The social invisibility thesis is that (1) darkness of skin is a decisive and visible mark of social difference—inferiority, in particular; (2) social conditioning can change behavioral differences but not skin color. While it seems to me clear that any denial of the significance of skin color in America flies in the face of reality, I do not think that the social invisibility thesis, which is not without some explanatory power, is satisfactory. For as well as the thesis might explain the attitude that academic institutions eventually adopted toward Jews, it does not begin to explain the perseverance of Jews in the face of hostility. After all, it is not as if Harvard simply had a flash of moral inspiration at some point and decided upon a policy of admitting Jews. They had been persistent at being a presence at Harvard, to the point of actually financing the appointment of a Jew in Harvard's Philosophy Department. A like claim can be made

---

[1]As quoted from Bruce Kuklick, *The Rise of American Philosophy* (New Haven: Yale University Press, 1977), p. 456. Kuklick writes: "Although the philosophy department invited Jews to study there, it made it difficult for them to later find jobs. Perhaps it's fairer to say that the philosophers did the best they could for men whose names would have invited discrimination in any circumstance, in the references written for Jews there is the unmistakable flavor of Lowell-like distaste for an unassimilated minority. [Ralph] Perry wrote of candidates that they were Jews without 'the traits calculated to excite prejudice,' having 'none of the unpleasant characteristics which are supposed to be characteristic of the race'; [James] Woods, that a candidate's Jewishness was 'faintly marked and by no means offensive'; [Ernest] Hocking, that a man was 'without pronounced Jewish traits'; and [C.I.] Lewis, that a young philosopher of 'Jewish extraction' had 'none of the faults which are sometimes expected in their cases.'"

for the success of Jews in the business world. I see no point in caviling over whether persistence paid off sooner than it might otherwise have done because of the truth of the social invisibility thesis, since persistence would require an explanation in any event. I believe that a satisfactory answer should locate the differences in the way in which we have characterized the difference between the Holocaust and American Slavery.

I argued in the last chapter (Section 16) that the Holocaust was not natally alienating, meaning that the practices and ennobling rituals constitutive of Judaism, and determining a Jew, survived entirely intact. The Jewish narrative was not lost on account of the Holocaust, even if it was rejected by some, questioned and revised or expanded by others. The practices and the narrative belong inescapably to Jews. No one else can lay claim to them, even if some Jews reject them.

In an insistently hostile society, there is no better way for the members of the targeted group to shore up their self-esteem, and there is no better salve for the blows to their self-esteem, than a mode of affirmation that is definitely the group's own—socially unencumbered group affirmation, as I shall say.[2] (While I shall not have any reason to qualify the significance of Judaism as providing socially unencumbered group affirmation for Jews, I shall in the next chapter put the point in a larger context.)

Being a good Jew from the standpoint of Judaism most certainly had nothing to do with American values. It was a matter of observing Shabbat, kashrut laws, and so on. Not only did these traditions have nothing to do with American values, but they often set the Jew at odds with mainstream culture. Still, a Jew who did observe such rituals could take pride in being a good Jew in a society that was sometimes hostile toward him or

---

[2]In a world of acronyms, one could say SUGA. I shall resist the temptation to do so, though perhaps the acronym could not be more appropriate, given both the various ways in which we sometimes pronounce "sugar" and the role that I have assigned to socially unencumbered group affirmation.

her precisely because he or she was a good Jew. This is what I mean by socially unencumbered group affirmation.

At one time, at least, Jews ostensibly lived in two worlds: the American world-at-large and their own world, which was not in any way a mere shadow of the former. Their world had its own customs, precepts, and values, which were not derivative of American values. Accordingly, their world served as a source of self-esteem for its members that was completely independent of mainstream America. For Jews who lived by these customs, American anti-Semitism could not tarnish the fact that they were good Jews, no matter how painful to them the anti-Semitism was in other respects. For as I said in the preceding paragraph, sometimes a Jew was despised precisely for being a good Jew. And this he or she knew.

Quite simply, if the Holocaust had been natally alienating, Jews in America would not have had socially unencumbered group affirmation to sustain them in the face of American anti-Semitism.

I believe that the phenomenon of socially unencumbered group affirmation is a vastly more satisfying explanation than the social invisibility thesis. Nothing better sustains a person in the face of hostility than affirmation from a source with which that person profoundly identifies. Nothing better underwrites a person's overall self-esteem than affirmation from such a source. The phenomenon of socially unencumbered group affirmation sheds considerable light on precisely the matter that the social invisibility thesis leaves us groping to understand, namely, what gave Jews the wherewithal to persevere in the face of adversity? Indeed, the affirmation phenomenon may very well take the mystery out of their doing so in a more general way, since the account applies across cultures. Beyond that, the thesis is compatible with Jewish self-hatred briefly discussed previously (Section 17).

Again, let me repeat that I do not maintain that the social

invisibility thesis has no explanatory power at all, but only that it is far more limited in what it can explain than no doubt is initially thought. Another reason for wanting to look beyond that thesis for an explanation is that the Holocaust makes it unmistakably clear that Jews need not be all that invisible in a society. Jews who so proudly identified with German culture that they initially greeted the thought of their being murdered with extraordinary incredulity were rounded up and killed by the Nazis. The Nazis believed they could tell a Jew from afar—even an assimilated one. Yet their purported powers of discernment had nothing to do with skin color, certainly nothing as pronounced as the difference between blacks and whites. The problem, then, is that one cannot make too much of the invisibility thesis without making the Holocaust itself seem implausible. For precisely what the Holocaust presupposed is that unerringly, or very nearly so, a Jew could be distinguished from a non-Jew. And that would be false if the invisibility thesis were as potent as is believed by those who put it forth as an explanation for the social difference between blacks and Jews. Even if it is true that Jews have been more invisible in the United States than blacks, the case of Nazi Germany shows that this is at best a contingent truth rather than one stemming from a socially transcendent truth about Jews, as the invisibility thesis seems to imply.

19. Blacks

The explanation that I have offered of why Jews flourished in a hostile society runs into trouble if one supposes that Christianity is for blacks what Judaism is for Jews; for, given that supposition, then either blacks ought to have flourished too, or Judaism does not explain the flourishing of Jews. As one might imagine, I want to deny that supposition.

To begin with, it is not possible for Christianity to be for blacks exactly what Judaism is for Jews. There is essentially an isomorphic relationship between Judaism and the Jewish people, whereas nothing of the sort holds between blacks and Christianity. But this much is obvious. By way of response, it might be said that, first of all, Christianity has surely played a most affirming role in the lives of blacks; second, in order for that to be so, blacks need not stand in the same relation to Christianity as Jews stand to Judaism.

There is no gainsaying this point. A black who was a second-class citizen all week in the white world could be a first-class citizen in her or his house of worship on Sunday morning. A black who had next to no standing in mainstream America, who was yet a "boy" to whites half his age, could preside over hundreds as a bishop or a pastor. Blacks may not have the relationship to Christianity that Jews have to Judaism. But clearly they did not need it in order for Christianity to have a profoundly affirming role in their lives.

Unfortunately, what is overlooked here is not just that there is an isomorphic relationship between Jews and Judaism that does not obtain between blacks and Christianity, but also that Judaism has its own narrative, which significantly predates the American narrative and which is relatively unaffected by it. Thus, in a very real sense, Judaism was none of America's business. Except for objects to the nature of such practices, America was not in a position to pass judgment upon the ways in which Jews practiced and interpreted Judaism, nor to comment upon interpretive debates between Jews. America was simply not a part of the conversation. Jews and non-Jews both knew that equally well.

Not so with Christianity, however. The ways in which blacks practiced and interpreted Christianity were, indeed, open to critical scrutiny by white Christian America. Suppose that black Christians were to maintain that a worship service is truly edifying only if the preacher achieves a certain cadence in his preaching, the choir reaches a certain exuberance in its singing and the congregation rises to its feet and many "dance before the Lord." Looking on, white Christian America could firmly insist that an edifying worship service entails no such thing in any of these three categories. In such a case black Christian America would have no interpretive leverage whatsoever.

Neither would whites, it might be noted.

True enough, but need anyone be reminded that the discussion is not an instance of white Christians disagreeing among themselves, where all parties to the debate have at least the semblance of equal respect, but a case of black and white Christians disagreeing with one another, where the specter of racism casts a very long shadow? In a deeply racist climate, there can be no such thing as equal odds in a standoff between blacks and whites, whether Christians or not. Only if blacks had interpretive leverage would this not be so.

It is important to bear in mind the distinction between the interpretation of the Christian text and the practices of worship. Insofar as there is a difference between black and white Christians, it is with respect to the latter, not the former. This should come as no surprise. After all, in the context of Slavery, Christianity was certainly hostage to the interpretation of whites. As to black worship practices, had enough whites venomously ridiculed slaves for their manner of worship, the effect would have been devastating for black worship practices. It would have been devastating precisely because blacks lack the relationship to Christianity that Jews have to Judaism, a tie that would have effectively insulated them from white criticism. In general, however, whites thought it best to leave blacks to their own ways of worshiping. In view of these two considerations, although black Christian worship was, indeed, a source of affirmation for blacks, it did not amount to full-blown socially unencumbered group affirmation.

Whereas the narrative of Judaism made it possible, not just for Jews to do things differently than Christian Americans, but for

Jews to evaluate themselves by a narrative that was rather independent of the American narrative, black worship practices did
not yield a like narrative for blacks. Stripped of their worship
style, black Christians were simply another group of committed
Christians. For all of their finesse in applying oral and rhythmic
traditions to Christian worship, blacks in no way produced a
reading of the Christian narrative itself whereby blacks could be
good Christians in spite of what whites thought—and both
blacks and whites alike knew this to be so. Blacks merely produced a style of worship, which for the most part whites ignored; and an independent style cannot possibly be enough if it
is expressive of the selfsame narrative of one's oppressors. Supposing otherwise would be like supposing that transposing a
song from one key to another and playing it at a different tempo
amount to producing a new song.

Finally, on this issue, it might be said that perhaps the most
telling evidence that blacks left the Christian narrative unchanged is that they did not come to see American Slavery as an
indictment of that message. Instead, they metaphorically interpreted their lot through Christianity, seeing their own situation
as akin to the biblical story of the Children of Israel in Egypt.
But I would think that a message of love must ring fairly empty
when its messenger has enslaved one, claiming as evidence of a
right to one's obedience that very message itself. One might attempt to deflect the force of this observation by pointing to the
truth of the message itself. The response to any such move, obviously, is that surely black people ought not to have seen their
enslavement as a sign of the truth of the Christian message. And
if they did so, that, of course, would be damning evidence that
they were natally alienated.

I believe that one of the most immediate consequences of
deep natal alienation is that a people are left without some form
of socially unencumbered group affirmation. I do not claim that
a natally alienated people cannot come to have socially unencum-

bered group affirmation in the course of time, but only that they are without it at first. Yet I will insist that expecting a natally alienated people to acquire socially unencumbered group affirmation in the face of sustained hostility is rather like asking a child to flourish in the face of sustained and relentless parental abuse. The child might flourish, but doing so would be something on the order of a miracle; accordingly, it would certainly be understandable if the child did not blossom. What is more, just as there are no substitutes for parental love when it comes to a child's development, there are no substitutes for socially unencumbered group affirmation when it comes to a people's flourishing in the face of sustained hostility.

For in the face of sustained hostility, socially unencumbered group affirmation provides the psychological buffer without which the very marrow of a people's self-worth is destroyed or stunted. The self cannot withstand assault after assault upon its integrity unless it is reinforced by some form of unencumbered affirmation.

While I shall not argue the case here, it is worth considering as a suggestion whether the racism that blacks have suffered over an extended period has resulted in a high level of group dysfunctionality among blacks generally. We know that abuse can result in dysfunctionality, and that once in place dysfunctionality can operate independently of the factors that gave rise to it, resulting in harmful behavior in other areas of life. No one would expect an abused child to lead a spiritually whole life simply because the abuse has been stopped. Generally, therapy is necessary for victims of child abuse even to approach spiritual wholeness in their lives. Likewise, it is ludicrous to suppose that even if racism were eliminated, its absence would suffice for blacks to lead spiritually whole lives. Something analogous to massive therapy may be necessary; and it is not clear how one would go about achieving that. Let me be clear that the suggestion here is not that racism no longer exists, as it certainly does, only that in addition to racism, *but owing to it*, a measure of dysfunctionality on the part of blacks is operating against them.

Generally, what is considered dysfunctional behavior is adaptive under the circumstances that produced it and so bespeaks enormous creativity. The suggestion here assumes this to be so in the case of blacks. The problem, in the individual case, is that because of deep forms of emotional estrangement resulting from the evil circumstances endured, the person is not able to change her or his behavior in light of the change in environment. The suggestion assumes this to be so in the group case. Patterns of survival that are forged in heinous moral circumstances are not easily changed, a fortiori in the absence of the salve of unencumbered affirmation.

20.   Historical Contexts

This brings me back to Judaism. Have I, in fact, painted too rosy a picture of the power of Jewish narrative?

Judaism would lack affirming power for Jews but for its standing in Western culture; and it would almost certainly lack that standing were it not for Christianity itself. At one point, Judaism was but one religion among many. In fact, time was when its standing was on a par with that of Christianity and when Christian opposition to Judaism was rather on a par with Christian opposition to any other religion. Things changed with Christianity's ascendancy in the world—in Western cultures especially—and when its claim to being the logical successor to Judaism was rendered secure. Then Judaism's high standing and historical significance were inextricably tied to the fact that Christianity took itself to have been born of Judaism. However foolish Christianity might suppose it is for Jews to go on adhering to Judaism, Christianity cannot, without undercutting itself, deny that Judaism is a tradition of inherent value that is nonetheless independent of it. Christianity's acknowledgement of the independence of Judaism keeps the argument of this section consistent. The problem for Christianity has never been Judaism itself, but Jews themselves. The irony of ironies is that not even the Holocaust could destroy the place of significance that Judaism has in the Western tradition, though it could destroy the Jews themselves.

It is said that one mark of the adequacy of any account is its explanatory power. I believe that the account that has been offered of the difference between American Slavery and the Holocaust and, in turn, of the fact that Jews seem to have flourished, whereas blacks seem to have languished, is most illuminating with respect to recent tensions between blacks and Jews. Although they experienced it in radically different ways, both groups know what it is like to have the machinery of the state pressed into service against them, to have their personhood officially not recognized by the state, either as matter of strict law or common law practice. On that account one might think that the two groups would have been spiritual siblings. And for a moment it perhaps seemed that this was so, as Jews played a pivotal role in the civil rights movement.

A great many white youth, many of them Jews, participated in the sit-in demonstrations at food counters throughout the South. Many of those sit-in demonstrations would have been far less effective had it not been for that support. Jews put aside promising law careers to work for the NAACP, making a formidable difference in the NAACP's success in the courts. It would be foolish to say that without Jews the civil rights movement would not have succeeded. All the same, it is recorded in history that the movement succeeded in part through the help of Jews.

With hindsight, which is not always perfect, some may think that the Jews are open to this or that criticism. Some may think that there was maybe a little more paternalism than brotherhood on the part of Jews who participated in the civil rights movement. These charges, even if accurate, are nonetheless compatible with the truth that it was with good will that Jews gave of themselves. The changes certainly do not change the fact that the movement succeeded in part because of the help of Jews. Perfection is hard to come by. Fortunately, however, one need not be perfect if one is to make a difference for the better in the lives of others. No Jew was forced to give up or put off a promising law firm career in order to help in the civil rights movement. Paternalism, alone, cannot explain the fact that some did so. Good will must be part of the picture.

Following the civil rights movement, though, rather than forging an increasingly closer bond, or even strengthening what was there, blacks and Jews were increasingly at odds with one another. They disagreed most vociferously over affirmative action, with the NAACP pressing the cause and many Jewish organizations opposing it. In no time, a strain of virulent anti-Jewish hostility found a voice in the black community. The economic success of Jews was called to attention, and Jews were generally portrayed as exploiters of black people. Some of this hostility is simply anti-Semitism itself, but not all of it is such, though the other part undoubtedly stokes the flames of anti-Semitism. I shall refer to the hostility that is not anti-Semitic as simply anti-Jewish hostility.

This virulent anti-Jewish hostility in the black community is something new. My reasons for refraining from calling it anti-Semitism will become evident as we proceed.

Because so much has been made of the economic differential between blacks and Jews, it is easy to think that the source of the hostility is to be located right there. Jews have succeeded, whereas blacks have not: end of story. It is an explanation that Jews have found most disturbing—most offensive, to be exact. And understandably so. They have wondered how anyone can begrudge them their successes, given the evil of the Holocaust? And that blacks, of all people, should do so has been rather like having salt poured upon an open wound. Although I believe the source of this anti-Jewish hostility to lie elsewhere, an observation is first in order.

Life being what it is, I should think it next to impossible for blacks and Jews living in the United States to resist infection by the prevailing prejudices against each other. In this regard, neither group is in the position to take the moral high ground. Neither group can claim moral purity. When either group attempts such a stance, as if one were to believe that it has just landed on earth from another solar system, it is nothing other than a profound affront to one's moral sensibilities. I mean to show that there is a virulent anti-Jewish hostility in the black community. The reason, however, is not that I am of the mind that there has been no racism on the part of Jews against blacks. I no more believe that than I believe that there has been no anti-Semitism on the part of blacks against Jews.

21. Group Autonomy

I want at this point to introduce the notion of group autonomy: a characteristic of a group that is regarded by others as being the foremost interpreters of its historical-cultural traditions, it being understood that the aim of others is not to show that those traditions should be jettisoned by the group of adherents. It is possible to think both that a group should reject its historical-cultural traditions and that within those traditions its members are the foremost interpreters. It might be thought that Christianity views Jews in this Light: Jews are the authority on the Torah, say. From the Christian perspective, however, things have moved beyond the Torah. Group autonomy is quite compatible with outsiders' making a contribution to a group's knowledge of its historical-cultural traditions, so long as this does not happen often. Even then, there is a presumption in favor of the group's own account of its historical-cultural traditions.

Group autonomy takes the regard that we have for an adult as the authority on her or his life and generalizes that regard across a group. It is an insult to ask a person how she is doing if her remarks are irrelevant, because one has already formed an opinion and is unlikely to change it on the basis of her remarks. Not even good psychological therapy so radically ignores what is said. To regard people as an authority on their own experiences is part of what it means to respect them. If regarding the individual as an authority on her or his own life has indisputable value, then so must group autonomy. And if individuals want to be so regarded by others, so do groups.

I maintain that Jews have group autonomy and blacks do not. Or, at any rate, Jews have considerably more group autonomy than blacks. And, as one might surmise, I want to say that this is so because the Holocaust was not natally alienating. Let me quickly speak to two objections.

In claiming that Jews have more group autonomy than blacks, I am very mindful of the fact that others have supposed that they knew better than Jews what is good for them.[3] Indisputably, Western culture has often sought to interpret the history of its Jews. At this point, I could simply remind the reader that my claim has been a comparative one: Jews have enjoyed more group autonomy than blacks. But rather than being content with such a Pyrrhic victory, let me also point out that history itself places strong limits on reinterpreting Jewish history. The very birth and story of Christ are tied to some of those traditions being firmly in place. For instance, the lineage of Christ is de-

---

[3]On this, see the important work of Frank E. Manuel, *The Broken Staff: Judaism Through Christian Eyes* (Cambridge: Harvard University Press, 1992). Of course, in times past, as in the case of Martin Luther, it was often true as it is now that Christians became an authority on Jewish texts and traditions solely for the purpose of serving Christian ends. For instance, many fundamentalist Christians believe that the return of Jews to Israel will hasten the occurrence of the Second Coming; hence, it is for purely instrumental reasons that such Christians are committed to the existence of the state of Israel.

vout Jews, and the Jewish Passover is an integral part of the story of the last days of Christ on earth. Indeed, as the story of the Apostle Paul indicates, the supposed stubbornness of Jews toward accepting Christianity is in some instances tied to their piety in adhering to their own traditions. Christianity has certainly supposed that it knows better than Jews what is good for them. However, Christianity has very little latitude to change and reinterpret the Jewish traditions that were in place before Christ, since the very story of Christ presupposes that many of those traditions be unchanged. Christians can call Jews foolish for continuing, after Christ, the traditions in place before him. That criticism, however, is different from claiming that the Jewish traditions before Christ ought to have been other than they were.

Here is the second objection. Regarding the claim that Jews enjoy more group autonomy than blacks, I can imagine someone thinking that I am failing, albeit with good intentions perhaps, in my aim not to make any invidious comparisons between American Slavery and the Holocaust; for perhaps it is beginning to look as if the Jews did not suffer as greatly during the Holocaust as might have been thought.

Are we to understand the objection to be that the Holocaust was indeed the evil we take it to be only if Jews are experiencing equally the suffering that plagues any other people on account of having been the victims of a great evil? I should hope not; for by that objection we must dismiss the thriving of the Jews as a chimera of some sort. More poignantly, any such line of thought is open to the charge of inviting invidious comparisons. The Holocaust was no less than the evil institution we take it to have been. Just so, it was not evil in every conceivable way. No institution has that dubious distinction. More important, the accounts of group autonomy and of socially unencumbered group affirmation that I have offered are compatible with every dimension of evil, down to the last detail of horror, that is known to have occurred during the Holocaust. Neither requires that we redescribe any evil of the Holocaust in a more palatable way.

Now, like socially unencumbered group affirmation, group autonomy is not a consequence of flourishing. Instead, it enables us to understand more fully how it is possible for victims of suffering to thrive. More precisely, economic well-being does not entail having group autonomy and having group autonomy is compatible with the absence of wealth. Although many Jews arrived in the United States in a state of poverty, as I have noted, they nonetheless had group autonomy. On the other hand, successful black athletes and entertainers are, by any standard, an economically well-off segment of the American population. Yet, there is no reason whatsoever to believe that these blacks enjoy greater group autonomy than other blacks. It is not even clear that this economically elite group can be said to have it.

The thesis that blacks lack group autonomy is clearly compatible with the account of American Slavery that I have offered. It is, in fact, a consequence of Slavery. One would not expect a natally alienated people to have group autonomy, as one would not expect such a people to have socially unencumbered group affirmation. But it might help to flesh things out a bit.

Racism against blacks is the view that blacks are incapable of full moral and intellectual maturity. It is next to impossible to hold that view about a people while simultaneously regarding them as the foremost interpreters of their own historical-cultural traditions, the issue of natal alienation aside. Crudely put, racism against blacks is the view that if blacks have a history, they are not likely to have the intellectual wherewithal to comment authoritatively upon their history. And the persistence of racism in academic institutions until the early 1960s did nothing to undercut such a negative view of blacks. As an aside, since anti-Semitism is quite compatible with Jews' having group autonomy, we can see, at once, that it is a mistake to think that racism and anti-

Semitism amount to the same thing but take different objects. Anti-Semitism never denied the intellectual powers of Jews; rather, it called into question their wherewithal to be morally upright.

I suggest that some of the hostility on the part of blacks toward Jews is best explained by the differential between the two groups with respect to group autonomy, specifically blacks' envy of the group autonomy that Jews have. There are two morally esthetic reasons that favor this explanation. First is excusable envy, as when sharp and unavoidable displays of differences between persons are an acute reminder of an individual's real and severe inadequacy. A disfigured person might have a measure of excusable envy. We would understand that envy, although understanding neither justifies the envy nor makes it a feeling that a person should have no qualms about. And perhaps a person should take steps to avoid being in situations where such envy is brought to the fore. All the same, excusable envy is understandable. The person who is plagued with excusable envy is very different from the individual who is given to contemptible envy, that is, to being discontent simply on account of others having possessions that he does not have.

Excusable envy on the part of blacks owing to the differential between them and Jews with respect to group autonomy would thus be a more morally palatable explanation by far than economic differential for the hostility on the part of blacks towards Jews. For the latter puts blacks in a most untoward light, suggesting that they cannot be accepting of the good fortune of others. The hostility, then, is seen as coming from a morally repugnant attitude. By contrast, if the hostility is seen as coming from excusable envy on account of the differential in group autonomy, then the hostility itself will rightly be seen as yet morally repugnant, but its source will not be. And that difference is of no small consequence.

If, as I claim, blacks have very little group autonomy and Jews are blessed with an abundance of it, then we do have a significant differential between blacks and Jews that gives rise to understandable envy, given the assumption that group autonomy is a fundamental social good.

The second morally esthetic reason is this. The explanation of excusable envy owing to the difference in group autonomy is not an anti-Semitic explanation. It is not about Jews' having a corrupt character or any of the stereotyped traits. In fact, it does not entail a negative assessment of Jews at all. It acknowledges a significant differential between blacks and Jews without rendering a negative assessment of it. If the explanation is correct, we would have a case of hostility toward Jews as a people that is not tantamount to anti-Semitism. A rare case, but not the first. As mentioned earlier, opposition to Judaism by early Christians, before Christianity's ascendancy, did not amount to anti-Semitism.

There can be no doubt that this anti-Jewish hostility has fanned the flames of anti-Semitism among blacks. But it is of great importance for both groups to distinguish between the two, because the difference between the two attitudes is of considerable moral significance. Unlike excusable envy, the very idea of excusable anti-Semitism strains credulity.

The idea that it is the differential between blacks and Jews regarding group autonomy that accounts for some black anti-Jewish hostility accords well with another consideration. Allowing that Jews have flourished in American society, they are by no means the only ones who have done so. If it is simply success on the part of others that occasions hostility from blacks, then there is no reason why Jews should be any more the object of black hostility than, say, successful white America at large. And if the hostility is focused upon Jews, an explanation is in order.

Part of the explanation for the focus by blacks upon Jews cannot but be the point made earlier: Although it happened in radically different ways, both groups know what it is to have the machinery of the state pressed into service against them, to have their personhood officially denied by the state, as matter of either strict law or common law practice. Yet Jews have gone on to flourish and blacks have not done so. It is a difference that cries out for an explanation. Native Americans are another group of people who have had the machinery of the state used against them. And if they had gone on to flourish in the way that Jews have done, my view is that Jews would share the focus of blacks with Native Americans.

At first thought, economic success would seem to be the most obvious explanation, perhaps because economic differences are so visible and so easily quantifiable. But I have tried to show that there is in fact a more morally palatable explanation, tied to a less visible and quantifiable, yet no less important, characteristic, namely group autonomy. Indeed, I have suggested that it is not group autonomy that follows in the wake of success, but the other way around: It is success that follows in the wake of group autonomy.

I should like to conclude this chapter with a speculative thought. It would seem that one of the best ways to get others to respect one is to get them to respect the observations that one makes about them. For, psychologically, this makes it very difficult for them not to take one seriously when one speaks about oneself. Thus, it may be that one way for a people to achieve group autonomy in a hostile society is by becoming an authority on the things that the members of that society value. It may be necessary for blacks to take this course in the United States. It may be a mistake to think that focusing simply upon the black experience, by way of rap music or film or dance, will ensure the moral and political standing of blacks in oppressive societies. For these accomplishments, important as they are, do not suffice to command the respect of nonblacks. Those who would insist that the respect of nonblacks is entirely irrelevant fly in the face of the social reality that all human beings are quintessentially social creatures. Jews are not the exception to the rule here, for it will be remembered that, for better or worse, Christianity—and thus Western culture—is forced to take the Jewish narrative seriously, to at least some extent.

Regardless of the contributions that blacks in Africa may have made to the origins of Western culture—an issue on which I have remained silent—it should now be abundantly clear that Western culture need not ever acknowledge such contributions. The suggestion in the preceding paragraph points to a way in which blacks can command the respect of those in Western culture, whatever the received view turns out to be regarding the contributions of blacks to the origins of Western culture.

The Fate of Blacks and Jews

I believe that it is not possible for a people who have been profoundly oppressed to flourish as a group in a relentlessly hostile society—at least not in the absence of an independent narrative. While it should come as no surprise that I think this, in view of in the preceding chapters of this section, I have not fully supported this view. I want to do so now. Essentially, I believe the problem of cooperation is not unlike the famous prisoner's dilemma discussed in game theory.

22.   The General Problem of Cooperation

Very informally, the prisoner's dilemma is this. There are times when it is rational for two people not to cooperate, although for each the yield from cooperating would substantially exceed the yield from going it alone. The rationale for not cooperating, is uncertainty with respect to the other's actions: There is no way that either can be sure that the other will cooperate by doing her part. And if either does her part while the other does not, then the one who contributes her share will be worse off than if she had gone it alone.

For example, suppose that chicken is sold in Middle Town, East Town, and West Town only during the same hour of the same day; Middle Town is equidistant from the other two, and equally accessible from both. The vendor in Middle Town sells chicken at twenty pounds for ten dollars, two pounds for five dollars. Clearly, any two people who have only five dollars each are better off pooling their resources and making a single purchase of twenty pounds for ten dollars, then dividing the meat equally with the result that each goes away with ten pounds. This would be much better than going it alone. Suppose further, though, that each of the same two people lives in one of the two towns equidistant from Middle Town, namely East and West Towns. Each in his hometown can get four pounds for five dollars, the only price at which the vendors in East and West Town sell chicken. In Middle Town, the two buyers could get double the amount if they pooled their resources. The problem, though, is whether each stranger can count on the other to show up in Middle Town, although they have agreed to do so. If only one shows up in Middle Town, he will be worse off than if he had bought chicken in his hometown at four pounds for five dollars. Instead, the lone purchaser in Middle Town ends up with only two pounds, since the chicken vendor of his hometown will be either closed or sold out of chicken by the time he returns to it. Given the uncertainty, each might be better off buying chicken in his hometown. Yet both would be better off pooling their resources in Middle Town.

Among friends and family members who are on good terms with one another, cooperation is not a problem. The void of uncertainty is filled by the trust and affection that each has for one another, by their identification with one another, and by the delight that each has in interacting and participating in joint enterprises. It is known by all that each wants to be a part of the endeavors of the others. It will be noticed that I spoke of family members who are on good terms with one another. Cooperation, of course, does not follow simply in the wake of a blood relationship. Family members may despise one another.

The preceding point about the family and cooperation has bone-chilling implications for those who believe that ethnic or racial group membership, in and of itself, can serve as a basis for cooperation. Group membership, per se, can no more serve as a basis for cooperation than can family membership. And if there can be no cooperation among the members of a group, then it is impossible for its members to flourish as a group—at least not in the face of sustained oppression.

It is tempting to think that if a group is a victim of relentless hostility in a society, their common trouble can suffice as a basis for cooperation. For then, this line of reasoning goes, the members of the group straightaway have a reason for cooperating with one another, namely, to bring about the end of the hostility that each faces on account of belonging to the group. Although there are better reasons for cooperating, the foregoing consideration might be thought to be efficacious in motivating members of a group to cooperate. But in fact this line of reasoning is terribly flawed, as I shall show.

23. Neither Coercive nor Affirming Cooperation

If anything seems obvious, it is this: For the members of any oppressed group, a sufficient reason for cooperating with one another is the elimination of social hostilities that they must endure at the hands of the society that oppresses them. On this view, even if strong group identification is lacking, the very fact of their oppression should suffice to ensure cooperation among group members. This is the argument from social hostilities to cooperation. However, things are not always as they seem. As I shall show, the argument is defective; for the hostility of oppression is not sufficient to ensure cooperation among the oppressed. But first some prefatory remarks.

At the outset, it is important to distinguish between coercive cooperation and affirming cooperation. Suppose two complete strangers on foot are being pursued by a pack of lions. As it turns out they come upon a rowboat next to a river. However, the boat contains a large rock that neither can lift by herself, but they can remove it from the boat if they work together. So together they lift the rock out of the boat. Did they cooperate? Well, since they voluntarily did something together, one might say they cooperated. But now let us suppose that each of these two women, complete strangers though they may be, belongs to a social group that is known to despise the other. Were it not for their own desire to live, each would let the other die, if not attempt to murder the other. In fact, on reaching the other side of the river, each quickly goes her separate way only because the emotional exhaustion of the moment has overshadowed their hostilities toward one another.

Still, it is clear that we have cooperation of some sort in this instance. It is equally clear that this is coercive cooperation rather than affirming cooperation. The cooperation is coercive because it is the only way either of the women could avoid a grave harm to herself. What is more, each could plainly determine whether the other was doing her part in lifting the rock. There was not an ounce of trust involved. Neither would have been in any way willing to turn her back toward the other. Had the escape required that each perform tasks completely out of the other's sight, there would have been no escape. So this little adventure does not portend either good will or trust between the women. It does not foreshadow future cooperative adventures, in which each will identify with the aims of the other.

By an affirming cooperation, then, I mean cooperation between two or more individuals, involving trust, to achieve a common goal (that is, a good defined independently of avoiding some harm) with which each identifies, when each delights in contributing to the realization of this goal. Undoubtedly, coercive cooperation and affirming cooperation are opposite ends of a continuum. Hence, neither is an all-or-nothing matter. And it may very well be that except in rare cases, the forms of cooperation are mixed, although the cooperation may be considerably more toward one end of the continuum than the other. Nevertheless, it must be acknowledged that the distinction is of considerable importance, and that it is a mistake to suppose that all cooperation is of the affirming form rather than coercive. As a matter of logic, pure instances of coercive cooperation do not entail affirming cooperation.

With the distinction between coercive and affirming cooperation now before us, the first thing to be said is that when the only basis for cooperation between the members of a group is the relentless hostility of society, then that cooperation is coercive rather than affirming. It may be rare that such hostility is the only basis for cooperation. There can be genuine group identification, and so forth. But that is a different point. My claim is that if all that a group has in common is hostilities, then the cooperation among its members can only be coercive. The second thing to be said is that a group does not flourish if the only form of cooperation among its members is coercive. As shall become clear in the following section, affirming cooperation is indispensable to the flourishing of a group. A most natural response here, of course, is that, flourishing or not, coercive cooperation is better than no cooperation at all, as the case of the two women's escape from the lions makes abundantly clear. Perhaps coercive cooperation can be seen as a precursor to affirming cooperation. While almost any form of cooperation among the oppressed against their oppression is better than none at all, the truth of the matter is that cooperation—even of the coercive kind—does not develop out of oppression as easily as one might think.

Recall that in the lion story, coercive cooperation occurred only because each woman was in full view of the other and thus each could be assured that the other was doing her part. No trust at all was required, because the condition of mutual assurance, let us call it, was met. Meeting this condition was fundamental to the stability of their cooperative endeavor. The problem, then, is this: First of all, coercive cooperation works because the condition of mutual assurance is met, thereby dispelling any need for mutual trust. Secondly, hostility against a group does not eliminate the need for trust between members of the group. That is to say, widespread hostility against a group does not itself satisfy the condition of mutual assurance among the members of the group; accordingly, such hostility does not ensure the stability that cooperation requires. By itself, societal hostility does not render anyone in plain view of others. To be sure, it would be wonderful if the members of a victimized group could, simply on account of being such, trust one another. But this is not the case. And the existence of oppression does not stand in for trust, as it were.

Thus, suppose that some members of a victimized group discover that their mode of living and self-presentation renders them relatively, but quite significantly, immune to the hostilities that other members of the group must endure. And suppose further that if the individuals who enjoy this immunity were to devote their lives to eliminating the hostilities against the group, the individuals themselves would in fact be worse off either in terms of experiencing hostilities against the group or with respect to their own material well-being. Well, since these individuals can achieve either of these negative goals on their own, what rationally compelling reason, owing to the prevalence of hostilities against the group, can there be for those who enjoy this immunity to devote their lives to helping the group itself achieve this negative goal? The answer, rather pointedly, is that there is none.

True enough, they might need help in the future. But then again they might not. We live only a finite amount of time; and individuals may have excellent reasons for believing that their finite lives will be relatively free from the hostilities endured by most members of the group to which they belong. To appeal simply to the good of the group, when these individuals can have the good that the group seeks, and perhaps more, quite independently of the group, is asking such individuals to be self-sacrificing. And if the appeal is to sacrificial behavior, then societal hostility itself is not the factor that explains the cooperative behavior of these individuals. And that is contrary to what the argument from social hostility assumes. The assumption was that societal hostility could suffice to generate coercive cooperation even if could not generate affirming cooperation and even in the absence of self-sacrificing behavior based upon strong group identification.

Without a doubt, it is a good thing for a group to eliminate societal hostility against its members. But if a group defines itself simply by reference to societal hostility, then it has no positive goals to give it direction. It has no positive goals for its members to identify with and take delight in realizing. In a word, it has no identity except as a group against which society displays such-and-such hostility. Thus, its success in eliminating societal hostility is problematic for the group. This remark also sheds light on the discussion in the preceding paragraph. If a group is defined simply in terms of the hostility against it and its efforts to eliminate that hostility, then to the extent that individuals can avoid that hostility independently of the group they have absolutely no reason not to do so. A person has no reason to cooperate with others in order to avoid societal hostility (or, for that matter, any harm) toward himself when he has every reason to believe that he is fully capable of avoiding that harm on his own. This shows that with respect to cooperation a group that conceives of itself entirely in terms of negative goals generates the very instability that the group would wish to avoid. The reason is that negative goals alone cannot generate either trust or the condition of mutual assurance. Cooperation in the absence of either of these is unanchored cooperation.

We can have stability with affirming cooperation because, by hypothesis, the point of cooperating is not that great importance is attached to avoiding a harm that, as fortune may have it, one may enjoy greater success at avoiding on one's own. If this is so, and the social hostilities are great enough, then one could understandably be moved to eliminate those hostilities from one's own life, however much one might identify with one's group. The point of affirming cooperation is to bring about a public good for the group itself. And while there can indeed be the problem of individuals' not doing their share, the difference is that the great importance attached to the good in question will not, in and of itself, be a reason for individuals not to cooperate with one another. The importance of avoiding a harm regularly inflicted upon most members of one's group can be reason enough to try to do so on one's own, notwithstanding that everyone else in the group is seeking to avoid the harm. By contrast, the very importance of achieving a public good that everyone else in one's group is aiming to achieve as well cannot in any way be a reason not to cooperate with anyone in one's group. It goes without saying that jealousy and any other unsavory motive can be a major obstacle to cooperation here. But that is true regardless of the form of cooperation in place. There is no need to be concerned with such matters here.

24. Cooperation and Having a Narrative

We have been discussing a group that conceives of itself simply in terms of negative goals—that is, of harms to be avoided. On my view, this is a group without a narrative. For a narrative, it will be remembered, defines values and (positive) goals. It also fixes points of historical significance and specifies ennobling rituals to be regularly engaged in by the members of the group—rituals that cannot be readily appropriated by others. We may say that a narrative defines a people's conception of the good, while providing significant historical reference points that often serve to anchor various values. In most cases, a narrative defines, albeit not exhaustively, the self-identity of the people to whom it applies. A narrative defines goods that are not reducible to individual gain. Suppose, for example, a people's narrative defines the existence of clean natural waterways as a good. It is, of course, possible for an individual to own a clean natural waterway. But the narrative does not claim that it is good for people to own clean natural waterways; it says that it is good that there be such waterways, which is a different matter entirely. Or suppose that a people's narrative says that it is good that the land should be adorned with pyramids. Here, too, each person could try to build more pyramids than the others. But, again, that is not the narrative. It does not claim that it is good that one person should have more pyramids than the next; it says that it is good that the land be adorned with pyramids. This is what is meant by the claim that a narrative defines goods that are not reducible to individual gain as such. I do not deny that narratives can be distorted, or that they can simply change. This latter narrative could no doubt come to be taken as a call for individuals to amass pyramids. Then we would have either a distortion or a change in the narrative.

On my view, simply avoiding societal hostility cannot properly count as a conception of the good. For one thing, it does not define positive goals. For another, it does not define any goals that are not reducible to individual gain. The only way we can obtain a purchase on the idea of a group's seeking to eliminate societal hostility against it is to say that, taken individually, enough of its members experience less and less hostility from the society. Whatever gains the group makes in this regard, each person certainly has a reason to secure this goal for himself alone.

The mistake is to think that avoiding societal hostility amounts to the same thing as a narrative or that it can properly count as a conception of the good. The common endeavor to avoid societal hostility cannot be an adequate basis for the self-identity of a people, though it may very well serve as a catalyst for forging self-identity among a group. It is the belief that it can do so that surely makes mysterious why there cannot be affirming cooperation given the fact of social hostility.

It can come as no surprise that only a people with a narrative can flourish in a hostile society, because only a people with a narrative can engage in affirming cooperation. A people with a narrative identify both with one another and with shared positive goals. Moreover, they take enormous delight in having a hand in the realization of these goals. Indeed, they great take pride in contributing—contributory pride, as I shall call it—to the realization of these goals. Each need not be concerned to do everything; it is enough that each wants to do something or the other. That individuals take great pride in contributing to the realization of the narrative's goals is of considerable significance. This factor speaks to a number of issues at once. It resolves the problem of the absence of trust in situations like the prisoner's dilemma; it eliminates the need for some form of threat as a means to securing cooperation; and it explains why individuals do their part, though they could enjoy the realization of this or that goal without doing so. The mere endeavor to overcome societal hostility cannot generate the same sort of contributory pride because, as I have just noted, that endeavor cannot be an adequate basis for the self-identity of a people.

The last concern is known as the free-rider problem. Why would anyone use his resources to secure an end that does not contribute to his personal gain and that will be realized anyway, when he could enjoy those resources exclusively for himself? The answer is simply contributory pride. It is a fact that people do not always define the good simply in terms of themselves alone. This is often true of people when they are at their best. Without coming close to being a saint, people nonetheless have a more expansive view of the richness of life, even the meaning of life. If the free-rider problem is resolved, then the second concern is immediately spoken to. As for the first, recall that we have reasons to trust others when they give us reasons to believe that they would not harm us or that they would provide us with a good, although they could, without penalty and without being noticed, act in a contrary manner. When contributory pride is operative in a person's life, it is the reason for believing that individuals will do their part, though they could refrain from doing so without penalty and without being noticed.

Contributory pride is no more mysterious than pride itself, and the delight we take in general in doing things that reflect well upon our talents. Even when alone and there is no chance of being heard by someone, a person who can play the piano well wants to do so. The person could listen to a compact disk for a great performance of the concerto, but she takes delight in playing up to her level of competence. Likewise, we want our lives to reflect those values and goals that are dear to us, and it is a source of pleasure to us when this is so. Thus, like pride proper, contributory pride has considerable motivational force. Just as pride can move a person to perform to up to her level of competence, though this is of no consequence to anyone but herself, contributory pride can likewise move a person to do her part in the realization of a goal, though the project's success is not contingent upon her contribution and her failure to contribute would go unnoticed anyway.

It is the rare case when the success of a project is tied to the contributions of a single person. And this is well known. Yet people often feel very strongly about giving what they can. In some instances, peer pressure alone more than adequately explains such behavior. Few people are indifferent to its being widely known that they are not doing their part. Sometimes good old-fashioned guilt, or at least the desire to avoid it, explains such behavior. But sometimes it is simply the joy of being a part of the good that is motivating. Life being what it is, motives are not always pure. There can be mixed motives for doing things, but even so, one motive can be primary. It may have been enough to get the person to behave as she did, though other motives were operative. So, although peer pressure and the desire to avoid feeling guilty may be operative in a person's life, they are no bar to contributory pride as a person's primary motive for doing her part. I maintain that a great many cooperative endeavors among human beings cannot be explained in the absence of contributory pride.

25. Blacks and Jews

At this juncture, it is obvious that I have been alluding to the difference in the fate of blacks and Jews. And it will seem that I have painted a far too rosy picture of Jews and a far too bleak picture of blacks. I do not claim that blacks and Jews mirror the theoretical account that I have offered of the difference between a people with a narrative and a people without one in a hostile society.

As for Jews, insofar as the language of narrative applies at all, it is manifestly clear that it is understood differently by different Jews. There is Orthodox, Conservative, and Reform Judaism. And there are secular Jews. Some Jews think that the Jewish narrative entitles the state of Israel to the lands that it acquired during the Six Day War. Others have come to take a very dim view of that line of reasoning. But to say that a people have a narrative is not to say that they all subscribe to it equally, or that they all understand it in the same way, or even that they all accept it. Certainly the last of these cannot be true; for then it is not clear that any people could be said to have a narrative. In the real world, all that is necessary is that enough people who are self-identified as members of the group attach some importance to some definitive aspect of the narrative of the group.

Again, I do not suppose that every Jew is, for example, giving every penny of charity to Jewish causes. It suffices on my account that there can be rallying points for Jews: the Six Day War (1967) for some, saving Soviet Jewry for others, and so on. Even most secular Jews think that it is a good thing that Judaism is practiced, and would be moved to act on behalf of the Jewish community at large if being able to practice Judaism were under siege.

In any case, it can be debated to what extent the actual lives of Jews mirror the theoretical account I have offered of a people who have a narrative. What cannot be debated, though, is whether there is a narrative that belongs to Jews in the United States and elsewhere.

With black Americans, things are quite different. Do they have a narrative waiting, as it were, to attach itself to them? Does that narrative begin with Africa? Or are the shores of America where it must begin? And if there is a narrative waiting in the wings, will black Americans embrace it? Was there a narrative that is now lost forever? Can blacks create a narrative for themselves? And if they can, does it really matter whether that new narrative reaches back to Africa? I do not know the answer to any of these questions. What I do know is that skin color does not make a narrative. If racism should be entirely eradicated tomorrow, most blacks would have next to no reason to identify with one another qua being black; for there is no narrative, and hence no conception of the good, to which blacks are heir, that the demise of racism would make abundantly evident. Not so if anti-Semitism were to be entirely eradicated tomorrow.

To be sure, having an enemy can be a galvanizing force. I have hardly denied this. Whatever significance the establishment of the state of Israel in 1948 has had for Jews, there can be no question that the occurrence of the Holocaust has given Israel a spiritual significance for many, many Jews that goes well beyond anything that it would have otherwise had. It is that spiritual significance that explains why the Six Day War was a rallying point for Israel. Yes, a common enemy makes a difference. But that can be no substitute for having a conception of the good. Indeed, it is a conception of the good that fixes objectives quite clearly in the case of a common threat. A narrative points to what differences can be put aside in times of crisis. In spite of the many differences between them over how to interpret the narrative, Orthodox, Conservative, and Reform Jews all rallied in support of Israel during the Six Day War.

I have asked whether blacks can create a narrative for themselves. Of course they can. Suppose the vast majority of blacks were to engage in various practices that they passed on to the next generation and the generation after that. And suppose that stories were attached to these practices. Malcom X led blacks out of one destitute state, and Martin Luther King, Jr., another, and Harriet Jacobs yet another. Naturally, Frederick Douglass and Marcus Garvey would have to be included. And suppose, further, that the writings of these individuals were elevated to the status of sacred texts, which black children ritualistically studied to find answers to questions past and present. Present blacks would be choosing for the well-being of future blacks. It would take many generations, but in the fullness of time, blacks would come to have a narrative bestowed upon them. That narrative need not have its beginnings in Africa. I am not concerned here to debate whether the black narrative should begin in Africa. Rather, I point out that it possible for blacks in America to have a narrative that takes as its starting point the shores of America. What is more, Christianity could be a fundamental part of that narrative, though not Christianity simply as it is interpreted by Western culture. There would have to be substantive rereadings of various passages in the Christian text. Such rereadings could be anchored, for instance, by the writings of a Frederick Douglass or a Harriet Jacobs or a W. E. B. DuBois.[1] These things, I should think, are very much worth knowing. There is still the further question of how much unencumbered affirming power the narrative would come to have. I do not know the answer to this question.

I should like to conclude this book with a most profound point about human beings. In Western culture, much is made of having the freedom to choose, the ideal being something like each defining herself or himself de nouveau. Of course, no such thing actually happens as we are much too influenced by our environment for that. What I would like to draw attention to is that in general a people do not choose their narrative. They may shape and refine it. They may even reject it; but in general they do not choose it. Yet in a hostile society nothing may be more important to a group's salvation than its members' having a narrative that they were not initially free to choose and that others not belonging to the group cannot appropriate. For in the face of the systemic hostility of oppression, there is no substitute for the socially unencumbered group affirmation that a narrative provides its people. This tells us what each of us knows in our hearts only too well, namely that there are goods that must be in

---

[1]Or Cornell West. See *Prophecy Deliverance!* (Philadelphia: Westminster Press, 1982). West is emphatic about Christianity playing a central role in the endeavors of black people to flourish. He may be right about that. I insist only that as Christianity is presently understood, blacks do not have an isomorphic relationship to it; therefore, Christianity as presently interpreted cannot be the linchpin of a narrative for black people. As I have already indicated in the text (Section 24), of course, there could come to be a form of Christianity to which blacks held an isomorphic relationship. West may mean to move in this direction. I do not see that he has yet done so.

place in our lives very early on if our living is to have direction at all, and if we are to have a measure of immunity against the vicissitudes of life. First and foremost among these is unconditional affirmation. There are many things that we can meaningfully choose from the outset of our experiences. Unconditional affirmation, however, is not among them.

In this work, I have tried to bring out the structural differences between American Slavery and the Holocaust, and the ways in which those differences have gone on to affect the survival of blacks and Jews, respectively. I have not aimed to minimize the horror of either institution; and I believe that all I have said concerning the survival of each group is compatible with every detail of horror that each group had to endure. I conclude with an observation of similarity rather than difference concerning blacks and Jews, namely that because both have had the machinery of the state pressed into service against them, the issue of trusting others looms large in the lives of each. Indeed, it is an issue that Jews and blacks must face vis-à-vis one another.

Now, I believe that it is not possible to have a just claim to the trust of those who have been egregiously wronged—at least not in the absence of having profoundly wrestled with their suffering. I have tried to explain the flourishing of Jews after the Holocaust without resorting to anti-Semitic notions; and I have tried to explain the shortfall of blacks, notwithstanding the many years after Slavery, without resorting to racist notions. This needs to be understood by all, perhaps most of all by those about whom this book is written. The failure to do so makes us unwitting accomplices in the *demise* of the other. And that would be worse.

Name Index

Subject Index